Thorns On The Rose

One woman's journey to survive disappointment, disrespect and divorce after fifty

Rose Reid

Afterword by Susan Gillpatrick,
M.ED., LPC, CTS, CATSM, CEAP

Ideas into Books®
W E S T V I E W
P.O. Box 605
Kingston Springs, TN 37082
www.publishedbywestview.com

This book is a work of fiction. Names, characters, places and incidents either are products of the author's imagination or are used fictitiously. Any resemblance to actual events or locales or persons, living or dead, is entirely coincidental.

© 2014 Rose Reid
All rights reserved, including the right to reproduction, storage, transmittal, or retrieval, in whole or in part in any form.

ISBN 978-1-62880-041-8

First edition, July 2014

Cover design by Kathy Carmon Tobey.

Digitally printed in the United States of America on acid free paper.

Dedicated to those for whom the shoe fits...

Prologue

APRIL 18TH, 2007

As I sat on my youngest sister's sofa, sobbing uncontrollably and writhing from the pain coming from somewhere inside my chest, I couldn't bring myself to tell her why I was having this delayed reaction to the events of the last 27 years. When we shared a room as children I was usually the one to comfort her after she suffered anything from a spill on her tricycle to a broken heart after the homecoming dance. Tonight, she was trying to be there for her big sis, but I could tell she felt helpless. She had never seen me like this. I had never been like this.

Nothing in my background had prepared me for this day. Through the years I had remained completely pragmatic when it came to love (my consumption of juicy pulp romance novels notwithstanding). I certainly had my share of suitors back in the day, but none of them gave me that silly schoolgirl feeling I always assumed would sweep me away when that special time came. Friends warned me that my cool detachment and odd working hours had catapulted me into "hard-to-get" territory, but I was nonplussed. I was mature enough to know that if that special feeling wasn't there, the relationship wasn't meant to be. If that made me hard-to get, so be it.

Being perceived as hard-to-get is like catnip to the average male who enjoys the pursuit more than the capture. Proof of that theory came when I had just turned twenty and was working as a waitress at City Café.

I hadn't poured a cup of coffee for my first lunch customer of the day—a handsome helicopter pilot—before he asked if I was seeing anyone. I told him I wasn't at the moment but that I didn't discuss my personal life at work. He asked me if we could talk about it over dinner the following evening. Intrigued that he was an out-of-towner and sophisticated enough to call the evening meal dinner, I told him I wasn't available on such short notice. We agreed on lunch sometime next week. Lunch turned into dinner and we became, what is called today, an item.

Charlie Bertrend and I dated all that summer as work on the big oil pipeline through Macon County progressed and he flew crews from Louisiana each week to engineer the project. He was relentless in his pursuit. Flowers, long-distance calls and exciting flights in the company plane to romantic getaways on the coast were just a few of the treats Charlie had in store for me each weekend.

It was heady stuff for a small town waitress who had to quit school to help her parents make ends meet. Still, for all his efforts, I must not have been *that* attached to him because I didn't shed a tear when he suddenly stopped calling for three months over the winter. I assumed he had met someone else while on assignment in another state. I could just hear him asking the waitress in the next small town: "Where have you been all my life?"

I stayed busy and stayed out of his way. He didn't come by the café for coffee and I didn't drive by Ellington Motel to see if his car was there. It was though he checked out of my life the day he checked out of his room.

By spring, when Charlie showed up at City Café with flowers and a diamond engagement ring large enough to catch the reflection of the surrounding eight states, I was already dating someone else. My assumption was apparently wrong. He hadn't found another girl in another town as I had imagined, but was busy traveling with his boss. He claimed that he had no time to call me before my shift started at the café each afternoon. He was terribly upset at the misunderstanding but I gave him a hug and asked if we could still be friends. No hard feelings. No tears. No heartbreak for me, anyway. It was for the best. While I did enjoy his attention, his sweeping romantic gestures and gentlemanly demeanor, I wasn't *in love* with him and true love and a real connection were what I longed for.

I was devastated a few years later when I learned of Charlie's death. He crashed his helicopter during a storm while trying to rescue six oil rig workers in Louisiana. Everyone on board was killed and it was a big story dominating the evening news. The yellowed newspaper accounts of the tragedy are still in my scrapbook. I can't help but think that if I had been more mature when I met Charlie, I would have appreciated the affections of such a strong, brave and selfless man and might have said yes to his marriage proposal. I've learned the hard way that there are few men like him around these days.

Unlike so many of my single friends at work whose only goal in life was to walk down the aisle and have a house full of kids, I never fretted over my unwed status as I celebrated birthdays in my twenties, thirties, and even my forties. I was busy with my work, my projects at home, my friends and family. I always had a small nest-egg in the bank and food on the table. I clipped coupons and scouted the newspapers for garage sales and flea markets where I could find bargains to furnish my little cottage, a home I had worked hard to pay off in just a few short years. My mother lived with me after Daddy died. My sister and her daughter moved in after Mama passed away. There was never an empty house when I came home from work late at night. When Sis would go on a long weekend trip, I relished my alone time. Soaking in a hot bath and relaxing with a New York Times bestseller or spicy romance novel was my idea of the perfect Saturday night. Back then, I knew exactly what psychologists meant when they talked of someone being comfortable in their own skin because I certainly was.

On this particular spring night, however, my skin was crawling. I wanted to jump out of it. I wanted to be anyone but me. I wanted to be anywhere but here. I wanted to climb into a time machine and jet back to an era when all I had to think about was keeping my glazed-over eyes focused on auto parts passing by on a conveyor belt. Good old, mindless, widget-watching. That's what I needed right now. Something predictable—unchanging—that's what I needed to numb this pain. I didn't trust myself with anything more stimulating than that. Why can't I stop crying? Oh God! Please help me! Why won't this horrible pain in my chest go away?

My sister became concerned when my hard sobbing hadn't subsided after nearly eight hours. She was talking to someone in the kitchen and when she hung up the phone, she brought my purse and jacket into the living room where my red and swollen face was buried in the sofa pillows. Maybe I was trying to smother myself. I don't remember.

"Sit up, Rosie. Now, drink this glass of water for me. Can you sit up to drink this?" I shook my head 'no' for fear I would choke on the water between sobs. I guess that proves that I was in some small way concerned about self-preservation.

"Okay, then, stand up and I'll help you with your jacket. We're going to the emergency room."

The hospital we went to is staffed around the clock with emergency care professionals in every discipline. On this night, my thoughtful sister was prepared to hear anything from "She's having a heart attack," to "She's going insane."

I was taken to a quiet room immediately upon our arrival at the emergency entrance. No waiting in the lobby, no filling out paperwork. I was crying at a fairly high decibel level at this point and I'm sure the admissions nurse thought it would be too upsetting to the other patients to have me out there in this shape. Once settled in my room down the hall, nurses worked quickly to get me on a gurney, help me into a hospital gown, and check my vitals. A young doctor came in with a stethoscope to listen to my heart. He shined a bright light through the tears in my bloodshot eyes to check the pupils.

Still sobbing uncontrollably and all the while asking God to help me stop, I never questioned my sister's decision to bring me to the emergency room. I had lost the desire for any control over my life at this juncture. A young nurse with the face of a cherub was my next visitor. She wore latex gloves and was carrying test tubes and one of those rubber band things they use when they want to take blood.

"Hello Rose, honey! I'm gonna need you to give me your arm here for a minute. I need some blood now, will you help me?" She had a soft, high voice and dimples. She smiled when I turned to face her.

"Oh my goodness! You're really a pretty lady, Rose," she said as she looked into my eyes and prepared the instruments for her task. I hadn't looked in a mirror since the night before and the sight was pretty rough even *then* so I couldn't imagine why she would lie to her new patient.

"No, I'm not pretty! Not anymore! Why would you say such a thing! I know better than that!" I rudely shot back.

"Shhh, shhh. Now be still. I need to find a good vein, Rose. Now, I said that because I mean it. You're beautiful and we're gonna take good care of you tonight!" she assured me.

She slid the tiny needle painlessly into my arm and I watched the blood drain from the vein into one of several little glass vials she had brought in with her.

"I've begged God to help me stop crying," I said, trying to explain myself. "I can't stop. I just want to stop…I just want to…" I wanted to spill my guts instead of my blood to this kind woman.

"I know, I know, honey," she interrupted. "Everything is going to be fine, Rose. We intend to find out what's going on and you'll feel better in no time at all." With that, the sweet nurse with the tender bedside manner bandaged my arm, fluffed my pillow and covered me with a warm blanket. When she left, it was as though her comforting presence had helped me turn a corner. The sobbing suddenly subsided. Now, if only the tears would stop rolling down my cheeks. I could breathe normally now and that was a relief.

Two older nurses came in next. One had a clipboard They both carried latex gloves. Neither was wearing a smile. "Rose, we need you to stand up for us and bend over the bed." I couldn't quite understand this odd request, so I asked her why. Was I getting a strong shot?

"I'm sorry to have to do this, but we're required to do a full body cavity search for drugs before you're admitted into this area of the hospital," she sternly explained. There was a moment where we all just stared at each other. I decided to break the uncomfortable silence with a nervous chuckle.

"Well, it couldn't be much worse than the humiliation I've already suffered this week, so have at it!" I smiled through blurry eyes.

They didn't react although I would imagine if full body cavity searches were a nightly occurrence for this team, they've heard it all. As I bent over the bed in a drafty, backless, hospital gown to suffer this, the worst of all indignities, the tears stopped flowing long enough for me to have a little *Come-To-Jesus* meeting with myself.

The emotion my sister had tried to bring out in me—anger—was starting to surface. It was something I so desperately needed to feel. I couldn't believe that it had come to this. Miss Rose Reid from one of the most respectable, decent families in the county was being treated like a criminal. After a lifetime of cleaning houses, working at factories and waiting tables—that young, fresh-faced girl, who the customers at City Café called "Sweet Rosie," was now a fifty-something woman at the bottom of a sad heap.

If being put through this routine had been the consequence of something illegal, a meth raid on my home or the theft of cocaine from a Mexican drug cartel, perhaps I would understand. But this predicament was not of my own choosing. I felt like saying "Lady, if I *had* good drugs they'd be down my throat and not up…well… *there*… after what I've been through." But, when a nurse with cold hands is behind you with a search light and a jar of Vaseline, you don't make jokes like that. It's almost like kidding about a bomb at the airport.

I'm not the shoe bomber, or the underwear bomber, or the Uni-bomber. I'm a good woman who, after five decades of a hard-knock life, is finding herself homeless, jobless, loveless and hopeless. I'm a woman who, after living a perfectly healthy life, has never spent a single day in the hospital. On this night, however, I'll be the guest of these nice folks at this wonderful facility.

They're checking me into the mental health wing for observation since they're as stumped as I am about why I can't stop these tears. I'm in too much pain to be embarrassed about it all now. I just want some of these experts to tell me why I allowed this to happen. I want them to help me understand how a strong, independent woman who waited until age 42 to fall in love and get married finds herself with nothing when it's too late in the game to start over.

I was released the next day after meeting with a gracious and caring counselor who assured me that while I still had my sanity, I was suffering the symptoms of severe emotional abuse which can have lingering effects long after the victim has removed herself from her abuser. In therapy, I learned there would be no overnight fix for me. Even the finest surgeons at the finest hospital would not be able to mend this gaping hole in my heart—the heart I had protected for so long.

Since that night, I've figured out on my own that while my heart continues to mend, it is still a mended heart with all the weak spots and fissures of a delicate piece of lace that has been torn and sewn back together. My heart may never be as strong as it was—*ever again*.

That just means I'll have to try harder to protect it next time—if there is a next time. Thus, the journey of an older and wiser Rose begins.

But first, let me share with you how I arrived at this place....

Some grumble because roses have thorns—
  I'm thankful that thorns have roses.

— *Unknown*

The Budding Rose

It was money, not love that was in short supply when I was growing up. Burtram and Evie Reid had ten children. I was next to the oldest of five boys and five girls who were all well-behaved and respectful of their elders. Before I was born, there was another sister Justine who died of polio when she was only six. It was the first polio death in Macon County at the time and it made headlines in the community newspaper. Back then, polio patients were perceived by the public almost as lepers, in the same way AIDS patients were treated in the early eighties. People were reluctant to come around a home where anyone had polio. They didn't know enough about it and were reacting out of fear—sometimes leaving those who were dying of the disease isolated and terrified.

Mama told us all that little Justine tried to be brave and selfless as she lay dying in the back room of our drafty old house on College Street. Her last words on this earth were "I'm not afraid, Mama, don't you worry about me." Justine didn't think of herself. At such a young age, this child's final concern was about the feelings of those she was leaving behind.

Daddy was a house painter but not just any painter, I'm told. He was the best at what he did and had all the work he could manage at any given time throughout the county even though he made less than minimum wage. Mama had the hardest job any woman can have—keeping house and raising ten children on mere pennies. As we all know, there's no check coming in for the endless shift of mothering. Mama always told us there was no dishonor in being poor, but being poor and *dirty* was a disgrace indeed. To Mama, cleanliness was the first order of business when it came to keeping house for a big family.

Simple Abundance

Payday was every Friday and as a treat for all of us, Daddy would stop by Smith's Grocery and buy an enormous can of Vietti Chili and a fresh loaf of bread. He'd have the butcher slice off a big hunk of fresh bologna from the deli case and sometimes he'd bring home a little something for dessert. It wasn't a healthy feast by today's standards, but it was certainly a filling one with leftovers that stretched well into the following week for our brown bag lunches at school.

We always had food on the table since we had a big garden and fruit trees in the yard. Mama canned dozens of jars of fruits and vegetables, pickles, jams and jellies. Our clothes were old, but they were clean and neat—a point on which Mama refused to compromise. I had one pink cotton dress that I wore every day to school the year round. In the winter, I slipped a cardigan over the short sleeves and donned knee socks or thick tights for warmth. Each afternoon when I walked in the door, Mama would tell me to go straight to the closet and hang that dress so it would be fresh for the next morning.

Our first chores upon returning home from school were to prepare for our next day. That meant rinsing out our clothing if needed, shining our shoes, and of course, doing homework. Funny how when you have no comparison, you don't realize you're part of a family with limited resources. We had food, a home, clothing and two great parents who loved us. We simply didn't have a lot of the extras and sometimes that alerted people in the community that we could use a helping hand.

Some friends of mine who worked at the school became aware of my lack of clothing options when they noticed I was wearing that pink cotton dress in the cold winter months. They thoughtfully and discreetly gifted a closetful of beautiful clothes that their older daughters had outgrown. Everything was just my size. For the first time in my life, I had a different outfit for each day, appropriate for each season. My brothers also benefitted from the generosity of this kind family who had two growing boys with clothes to share as well.

I was never embarrassed that I was "Second Hand Rose" as the song implies. Material things have never been a focus in my life. In fact, I'd rather shop in a consignment store than at any of the finest retail stores around. It causes me physical pain to pay more for an item than I have to and I'll search endlessly until I find the article I need at the cheapest possible price.

Notice how I said that I search for the article "I need." Mama taught us so much about discerning our *needs* from our *wants*. I do a lot of "Do I *really* need this?" soul-searching before I buy anything thanks to my frugal and wise mother.

A Restless Heart

What I really *needed* was to get out of town with my friends as much as possible back then. I was bored and with no football games to attend in the spring and summer, Lafayette was not exactly the fun and sun capital of the world for an antsy teenager.

On Saturdays, a car load of us would check out parties or picnics at the lake near Gallatin or Old Hickory. One of my friend's parents had a boat and they would take our group out on that occasionally. It seemed there was never a shortage of harmless, fun things to do if a body of water was involved and the sun was shining. We were young and were determined to enjoy every minute of our summer.

One weekend, a friend's cousin in Fountain Run, Kentucky was throwing a huge birthday party with swimming, music, food, and dancing. It promised to be a great time with a new crowd—just hanging out and taking in some different scenery. Since Lafayette is practically right on the Kentucky and Tennessee border, Fountain Run is less than thirty minutes away and all the parents were okay with us making the small trek north for what promised to be the coolest party of the season.

The event was on private property, in an area with beautiful dogwood trees, a waterfall and a swimming hole complete with a rope swing. A fabulous band, unexpectedly good for a high school garage-group, belted out the latest Beatles hits. Burgers, ribs and chicken smoked on the barbeque as couples held hands and talked or danced. Some brought their bathing suits and played volleyball in the water until sundown. Tiki-torches and a big bonfire gave the area a golden glow and warmed the late-evening swimmers who were chilled to the bone.

Once darkness fell, everyone divided into their familiar little cliques and the group having the most fun was made up of about eight or ten boys who looked to be a bit older than the rest of the crowd. One of them had a moustache that was too thick for the typical baby-faced high school boy and he was holding court with the apparently hilarious stories he was telling. Our little group of girls was particularly interested in these guys. It was so exciting to meet people who weren't from Macon County—so refreshing to get a new perspective. Maybe these guys were college frosh from the University of Kentucky! They were all neatly dressed and kept sneaking a look in our direction. We were impressed.

I was the youngest in our group of six girls, but my friends swore not to reveal my secret. Our host for the party was kind enough to take us over and introduce us, once she sensed that we couldn't take our eyes off these rock stars. We were right in our assumption. These guys were all from the University of Kentucky. One of them looked vaguely familiar and as I asked him if we had met before, I immediately cringed at how my question sounded like an old pick-up line. He laughed at my bold approach and told me that our families had known each other a long time, but that I was too young to remember. I remember thinking, well, that's just great. The best-looking guy in the crowd thinks I'm a baby. I certainly would have remembered *this* face if I had ever seen it before.

His thick hair kept falling onto his forehead and he had obviously developed a nervous habit of brushing it into place with his fingers as he talked. That jet-black mop, which he had grown slightly over his ears to resemble Paul McCartney's, sharply contrasted with his pale, smooth skin. His eyes were a striking blend of turquoise and gray and he had dimples and beautiful teeth when he flashed a broad smile. His shiny, black lizard cowboy boots had seen many miles but looked as though he had brought them to the party in his coat pocket. Everything about him was neatly tailored, clean and pressed.

"Clay is my name. Clay Hutchison," he said. "And you're little Rosie Reid." I blushed at being called "Little Rosie," because it erased all doubt that he knew my secret. I had been fifteen for exactly two weeks and was here with my eighteen and nineteen year old pals. I was so hoping to blend in with this crowd and be mistaken for a sophisticated, collegiate, woman of the world.

"Now, how is it that our parents know each other?" It was annoying that I didn't remember.

"Oh, your Dad did some work with me and my Dad on a piece of property we owned on Scottsville Road," he explained. "I think you had just started first grade and your Dad was talking about his little Rosie. He had to pick you up from school that afternoon and you sat in the corner and drew in your coloring book while we dry walled." Clay reminisced. "It was right before my senior year. Man, time flies," he said as he looked down at the melting ice in what appeared to be club soda with a lime.

"You're ten years older than me? That makes you twenty-five!" I said. Now I really felt like the child in the group.

"So, little Rosie can do the math," he quipped. "And, no, I'm not spending my life in college. I graduated a while back."

We all mingled and talked as the food was taken away and the dancing began. People were still divvied up into little groups. One of the guys took a deck of cards from his pocket and dealt a few hands of poker on one of the big picnic tables. Chuck, the University of Kentucky basketball recruit from Glasgow who came with Clay's group, held up an empty Coke bottle and smiled.

"Anybody for a little game of *Spin*?"

With that invitation, the six of us along with Clay's group and a few other singles who were wandering aimlessly, gathered in a circle in an alternating boy-girl-boy-girl pattern as Chuck placed the bottle on the pavement, gave it a whirl, and spewed out the play-by-play like the man at the roulette wheel in Vegas. The bottle landed on a giggling blonde and Chuck wasted no time with introductions. He went in for the kill with a kiss that seemed to last an embarrassing eternity.

Before this marathon kiss was finished, Clay took his spin. At exactly that instant, Chuck swung around from his embrace with the blonde and stopped the bottle with his foot, which left the tip of the bottle pointing directly at me. By default, I was going to be kissed by this grown-up, probably married-with-ten-kids man tonight, whether I liked it or not.

With the others in the group yelling "Whoohooo," Clay leaned over and planted an appropriately timed and gentle kiss on my lips as he cradled my head in his hands. He then made room to sit beside me, silently, as the game continued and everyone playing had been kissed at least once.

Hey, we were kids and it was an evening. Looking back, it was simply innocent fun and a great way to get to know the available men in our neighboring state.

It was a delightful time with fun people, but when my friends let me out at the front door in Lafayette around 11pm, I was exhausted. I'd been up since five that morning to work the breakfast shift at the cafe and had been going full steam at the party. I was simply too pooped to give a lot of thought to Clay. Besides, he was from a place in Kentucky I'd never heard of. I'd probably never see him again as long as I lived. I must admit, however, the memory of the tender kiss gave me sweet dreams that night.

Big Changes

By the time school started in the fall, I was busy with a homework load that was becoming unmanageable. I was juggling school with waitressing in the afternoons and something had to give. For me, waitressing was so easy it was like getting money for nothing. I had watched my parents struggle long enough and with three kids still at home, their money situation was only going to get worse as they aged. I quit school before my sophomore year and began my first full-time job as a waitress.

All of us were raised with a great work ethic which meant anytime I could work overtime, I did. With tips and my base salary of $35 at week at City Café, I made a nice living and had time after my 11AM to 7PM Monday through Friday shift to study for the GED a couple of years later. Getting my high school diploma had been on my mind since dropping out, and I was so relieved to check that goal off my list. I continued to live with Mama and Daddy, and that allowed me to open a checking and savings account to plan for what I knew what was going to be a happy future. During that time, many of my older girlfriends were graduating and getting married. Some had walked down the aisle before their senior year and were already expecting their first baby.

It didn't bother me that I was no closer to finding a husband than I was to winning the lottery. I couldn't have cared less. I had my independent life all planned out and landing a husband wasn't even on my list of goals. A few years later, I found the perfect little cottage for sale. It was a definite fixer-upper, but just my size and price range. My name was now on a deed and I couldn't believe my good fortune. My weekend mornings were spent in my flower garden in the spring, the vegetable garden in the summer, and on those warm, lazy afternoons, I could be found lying in the backyard hammock. This was life!

Changes

I was terribly disappointed when City Café closed in the early seventies. The Café was a fixture on the public square and one of the few places lawyers, politicians, blue collars and blue bloods could mix it up over a good cup of coffee and a plate of eggs, sausage and hash browns. I had grown up there. It was where I was working when I met Charlie, the pilot who gave me the wonderful gifts of my first airplane ride and my first taste of champagne. There were so many things those old plaster walls had seen and heard. It seemed to me that every photograph that Macon County Times Editor Charlie Gregory caught in his viewfinder included the backdrop of one of the tables at City Café. We would all have to get over it now. Our little piece of history was gone forever.

    I had to have a job and since there were only a couple of family-run restaurants in Lafayette and no openings at these establishments in the foreseeable future, I applied at the new plant in town that everyone was talking about, The Center Metals Company. It was dangerous work but I went into it without giving safety a second thought. I worked on a huge, noisy molding device and was required to wear ear plugs, protective goggles and heavy gloves. A leather apron protected my clothing from metal shavings and black oil. The top of the machine would open up like an astonished mouth and automatically slam down on a solid sheet of metal, turning it in to a small machine part. I had only a few seconds to reach inside this mouth mechanism and pick up the newly-minted part before the next sheet of metal slid under the giant stamping device to mold another one just like it.

This went on minute after minute, day after day and I had to pay attention to what I was doing or I could pull back a bloody stump. One worker did lose his arm up to the elbow. Many lost fingers. Those were really bad days when we heard about accidents happening on our shift. There but by the grace of God, as they say.

I was quick, safe, and capable with this arm-eating monster. I was good at what I did and even better at explaining these complicated machines, so management gave me a little promotion and asked me to train all the newbies coming in each month. That broke up the workday and interacting with people again made me feel that I was in my element. It was as though I was back at the job I missed so much—waiting tables and greeting all the friendly people at City Café.

When Center Metals moved to another country and made the automation transition to save on limbs and lawsuits, Carter Automotive, a carburetor manufacturing plant, moved in and employed hundreds in our hometown.

Our Mayberry kind-of-place with its highly skilled workforce could now rejoice that the economic devastation which followed the sudden closure of the nearby silk mill and the metals plant was a thing of the past. Fridays were once again called "payday" and the optimism was contagious; spawning new buildings, new businesses, and economic growth the likes of which our little county had never seen.

Rose Blooms

At age 32, I was still single and felt my life was just about as good as it gets. Maybe it was a throwback to my childhood when I had no comparison and didn't realize there were other worlds out there, but I was content. Daddy had passed away several years before and Mama moved in with me in my house. My free days were spent with Mama, my sister, and the new little nieces who brought me so much joy with their visits. The babies loved spending time with their Auntie Rose and I enjoyed spoiling them with my attention and affection. This was life on my terms and I loved it.

I had to be at work at 6:30 AM and the end-of-shift whistle blew at three in the afternoon. Work was such a no-brainer at Carter Automotive that I still had lots of energy when I got home to Mama who always had a delicious meal prepared and the house cleaned.

In the summer, we would throw some burgers on the grill and take a quick walk around the neighborhood for fresh air and exercise. In the winter, we'd each snuggle in a granny-square afghan on the huge sectional sofa to talk about our day or catch the latest episodes of Dynasty or Dallas. If there was nothing interesting on the tube, I'd lose myself in a romance novel until time for a hot bath and then I'd hit the pillow to prepare for the whole process to begin again the next morning at five sharp.

Social Butterflies

Occasionally, I would go out to dinner with a fellow who was metaphorically dragging a smoking parachute behind him from a failed marriage and that would scare me senseless. I simply had no time and even less inclination to waste a weekend hearing about someone else's relationship problems. I wanted life to be simple and free of drama.

Regardless of my fears, I did date frequently and even had a marriage proposal from a very nice, older, widower in town but I wasn't serious about him, at least not serious enough to give up my life and take on his. That's what marriage amounted to in my mind: sacrificing my independent life and glorious solitude to live 24 hours a day, seven days a week, waiting on a man hand and foot. To share my bed, my thoughts, my tears and my dreams with someone who had already lived four decades or more and was set in his ways, was more work than it was worth to me.

Even worse, in my opinion, would be marrying a man with an ex-wife and several kids. At my age, ending up with a divorced father with young ones still at home was a very real possibility—especially in a small town where guys marry their high school sweetheart on graduation day. I couldn't picture myself as a step-mom, although I love children. I just couldn't imagine what a pain it would be to have another woman breathing down my neck while her kids were visiting their dad in our home every other weekend.

I also found myself wondering why these men were divorced. What happened in the marriage that couldn't be resolved? Beware the divorced man who tells you his first wife tried to run him over with her Suburban. Marry him and you might soon find out why wife number one wanted to take such a drastic measure. The thought of all that drama made my stomach turn flips.

Yep. Taking on another woman's problems was not my cup of tea. I had relatively small issues that any single, working woman has on a day to day basis: a dead battery as I'm headed to work, a freezer on the blink, or a mouse situation in the basement. Nothing churned around in my mind to keep me awake at night. There was nothing wrong with me that a good book or a quick walk around the block wouldn't solve. Life was good just the way it was.

Then the call came in.

And You Are...?

I was reading with my feet wrapped up in a quilt on the sofa, so Mama scurried to the wall phone in the kitchen to answer. It was before cell service existed. There were no cordless phones and back then, North Central Telephone Cooperative charged big money for extensions in other rooms. The inconvenience of it all made for quite a workout for anyone who got a lot of calls but, thankfully, I didn't have to worry about that. Nightly telephone conversations were rare in my house because everyone in the family knew my early-to-bed, early-to-rise routine.

After saying a few words to the person calling, as she was known to do—carrying on conversations with people who had dialed the wrong number—Mama peered around the corner and whispered "It's a man who says his name is Clay Hutchison, dear." As I got up from my mystery novel to get the call, I was shaking my head as to why Clay—if it was the *same* Clay—would be calling me after all these years. Meanwhile, Mama looked even more puzzled than I.

"Why does that name sound familiar?" She had her hand over the receiver to mute her question.

"You and Daddy knew his Dad ages ago, Mama," I reminded her as I grabbed the receiver from her hand.

"Hello?"

"Hello Rose, This is Clay Hutchison. I hope you remember me. I met you at Sylvia Wilson's Fountain Run

Party when you were fifteen. It's been a long time, how have you been?"

It's been a long time? Are you *kidding* me? How about seventeen years? I was thinking that but didn't say it.

"Oh, of course, I remember. Spin-The-Bottle!" I chirped.

"Yes, a game I rigged so I could kiss you," he confessed. "Let's go to Lebanon to the new steak house." He wasted no time getting to the point of the call.

"Right now?" I asked, as I stood there in my faded, hole-y sweat pants and stretched black turtleneck.

"No, not right now. Next Saturday night," he laughed. "That is, unless your dance card is full then."

I paused, as if to look at my hectic schedule, and then gave him the answer.

"Well, Clay, you called at a good time. I've just canceled some plans and next Saturday works out just fine." I'm terrible at lying and was hoping I had convinced him that I wasn't a total loser who stayed home every weekend.

"Then it's a date," he proclaimed. "Next Saturday, I'll pick you up at your place at 6:30. You still live in the little house you bought across from the high school?"

"That's right. How did you know?" I was curious as to how a man in Who-Knows-Where Kentucky, who hadn't laid eyes on me in seventeen years, knew exactly where I lived.

"I have my sources. I'll see you Saturday night, Rose. I can't wait." He abruptly ended the call, barely giving me time to say a proper goodbye. I sauntered back to the sofa, scratching my head and trying to figure this Clay Hutchison guy. Am I nuts? I've just made a date with a man I haven't spoken to since I was fifteen. Then, the realization of what I had done hit me like a safe falling from a two-story window in a Road Runner cartoon.

Second Thoughts

Oh geeze, he's 42 now! He's got to be divorced, probably has kids, an ex-wife, the works. All my worst fears rolled up into one, surprising, mysterious stalker who knows where I live and that I'm single and not busy next Saturday. Oh *no*! What if he's still married and looking for a fling? What if his jealous, young, trophy wife shows up in her Suburban full of child-restraint seats and runs us both over in the driveway?

For the first time in a long time, I had trouble getting to sleep that night. I couldn't put my finger on it, but I'm sure it had more to do with fear than excitement over the upcoming date. Anyone I ever knew who also knew Clay had moved away to parts unknown. I couldn't call them and ask for the complete dossier on his life now.

Like Scarlett, I'd have to think about this tomorrow. As the auto parts go whizzing by on the conveyor belt, I'll figure this out. Right now, I need some good, solid, REM sleep that works wonders to unravel that sleeve of care that Shakespeare talks about. Heaven knows I have cares now.

The Rose and The Clay

Nothing about Clay Hutchison exuded money. Nothing he said, did, wore or drove said "Look at me!" Especially the vehicle he drove for our first date, an old baby blue, rusty and dented farm truck. I watched him from the kitchen window as he glanced at his reflection in the driver's side mirror and ran his fingers through that now slightly graying mop of black hair—a teenage habit that had now become a 'tic' of sorts, as I would later surmise. Someone told me at the Fountain Run party that when Clay brushed his hair from his eyes, it meant he was nervous. And he was nervous on this night so many years later. He couldn't hide it. I almost felt sorry for him. He was indeed as handsome as I remembered. It was as though time stood still for him. Except for the few areas of gray around the temples of his still-full scalp of glorious hair, he looked just as he had at the party when we met so many years ago.

Watching through the kitchen window as he made his way up the drive to the steps, I was stunned by those clear, sparkling turquoise eyes. I wondered what was behind those eyes. Why did he call me after so many years? What would we have in common? Why was I acting like a silly schoolgirl already?

I wouldn't know until much later, but this was a night Clay had planned for the entire *seventeen* years. I was his "dream girl" and, according to him, he felt he had won the lottery as he pulled in to the driveway to gather me for our first date. If I had known that night how he felt, I might have thought he was a stalker.

He was so bashful that those beautiful eyes darted from my face to the doormat and back again when I opened the front door. After a quick "Hi, how-ya-doin'-ready-to-go," he hurried me to the truck and helped me into the vehicle which was as neat as a working farm truck can possibly be, but still reeked of the unmistakable farm mixture of gasoline, grease and crushed corn. There were no stringent seat belt laws on the books at that time. A good thing, since this truck did well to have headlights. In a neat stack on the seat between us were some clues as to how this man spent at least some of his time. Perhaps from these clues I could glean something for the conversation mill. There were receipts from the feed store, a repair order for a tractor part, a pair of dirty work gloves, and a new box of worm paste for horses. There was a screwdriver, a couple of nails and a small tin of snuff. Yuck. I hope he doesn't dip snuff. That'll make for a nasty good night kiss.

It all added up to farming and as Clay climbed in and backed the truck out of the driveway, I began to worry about not being able to keep up with him in a conversation about his life's work.

It took approximately to the end of my street for me to realize that would be the least of my worries.

The trip to Lebanon from Lafayette is less than 45 minutes, but for me, a person who can't stand silence, those few minutes seemed like an eternity. I decided to break the ice with a few questions in hopes of priming Clay's conversational pump. I became Barbara Walters—asking about his college days, his work on his farm, his hobbies and friends. And, like Bab's worst television nightmare, I got one-word answers for my trouble. No details, no explanations. On the radio, the song "Like A Rock" was playing and I could relate. I was trying to converse with a stone. This was going to be a long night.

Check please...

During dinner at the Ponderosa Steak House, I kept stealing glances at my watch and listening in on conversations at nearby tables. I've always heard the cliché that you can always pick out the married couples in a restaurant—they're the ones not talking. Tonight, my observations were turning that theory on its ear. As Clay ate his steak in silence, I tuned in to the sweet discussion of an elderly couple who had obviously been married for many years. They were very animated as they chattered about the antics of their grandchildren and the upcoming birth of a great-grandchild. Their eyes sparkled and their joy was palpable.

What kind of turn had *my* life taken? I was on a date with one of the most gorgeous men on the planet and I was envious of a couple of octogenarian lovebirds cooing at each other in the next booth.

Following dinner, I had hoped that my host for the evening had planned a movie, a concert, or a trip to the comedy club in Nashville for our entertainment. At least I would get a break from doing all the talking during a show of some kind. Imagine my surprise when we left the restaurant and began to "ride around" the square in Lebanon over and over again like bored teenagers looking for action. I asked him what (the hell!) we were doing and he admitted that he just wanted to see the city since he hadn't been there in so long. He commented on the old theatre and how his parents used to go to movies there when they would come to town. He was upset that one of his favorite stores had gone out of business and was thrilled they had put some fancy new lighting on the square.

To say that this man "didn't get out much" was an understatement, but I was grateful for any small talk I could squeeze out of him. He did manage to tell me that he had never been married and had no children. But at this juncture, it didn't matter. I didn't care if he had ten kids.

This guy was a b-o-r-e. I began to feel extremely uneasy and at the same time, terribly disappointed that such a great looking, kind and gentle guy, was such an insufferable stick in the mud. Walking to my front door that evening, all I could feel was relief that this uncomfortable night was over. I couldn't imagine that Clay had a good time. I certainly didn't. I handed him my keys and he unlocked the front door and turned to face me.

"Oh, Rose, I had a great evening. You know I've loved you since the first time I laid eyes on you when you were that beautiful fifteen year old girl in Fountain Run. You haven't changed a bit. Are you free next Saturday night?"

I was stunned. Did he just say what I thought he said? That he *loved* me? That he wanted to go out with me next Saturday? Could I endure this much work again? This date had been like digging a well with a teaspoon. I had tap-danced, cajoled, fake-laughed and horse-grinned my way through this evening from hell and he wants to put me through it again next weekend? And it's no wonder! All he had to do was eat, drive and breathe.

My thoughts were running amok and he must have thought I had suffered a stroke as we stood there on the front porch. I said nothing, but simply stared into space trying to come up with a reason as to why we should never see each other again.

A Glutton for Punishment

Then he smiled at me, touched my face and burned through me with those dangerous eyes as he waited for my answer. Never before, and not since, has my mind turned such a somersault. He had worn me down. Against my better judgment, I said "Yes, it would be fun to go out next weekend, thank you!" I'm such a coward.

I didn't have the heart or the energy to ask him in for coffee. Besides, it was getting late and my proper southern manners taught me that nothing good can come from that anyway, especially after a first date. You have to watch out for the quiet ones or they'll get you all wrapped up in a make-out session to keep you from talking.

As he backed his old blue truck out of my driveway, I heard a hot bath, my soft cotton pajamas, and a carton of orange sherbet calling my name. I needed to treat myself for being the polite lady who had tried to be sociable with a man who had the personality of a wet mop.

I soaked in the hot water and allowed the bubbles and the steam to take me away from my troubles, but in my attempt to recount the events of the night, I almost slipped under the water—completely comatose. What have I done? I feel as if I've worked two eight-hour shifts with a highway paving crew and I've committed myself to going through all this *again* one week from now?

I was slathering on my vanilla-scented moisturizer and slipping into my fuzzy slippers when the thought occurred to me that perhaps I needed to give Clay Hutchison the benefit of the doubt. He was apparently nervous. After all, he did say he had loved me for so many years. But, what did he mean by *love*? What does *any* man mean by love when it slips off the tongue so easily on the first date? Yikes. So many years ago, he had "fixed" the outcome of Spin-The-Bottle like a mobster fixes a horse race but now we were playing an adult game. A normal adult throws the word *love* around like a manhole cover. One should be especially suspicious if it's one of only a *few* words a man has said all evening to a woman he hardly knows.

Then, my thought processes went in the other direction for no reason. Perhaps he's intimidated by me, I thought. To him, I'm a woman of the world—the one who got away and never looked back. That's got to be it. He was terrified tonight. He'll be back to his old self next week. We'll have a great time. With that all figured out, I drifted into a deep sleep. Being charming is hard work that I obviously wasn't in shape to do. It was definitely time to get the old dating muscles in training. Clay was worth a second chance—maybe even a third.

Gotta Organize The Sock Drawer…

As three more weekends and a few weeknights of dating turned in to almost a full month of "giving Clay a chance" to prove himself, my handsome prince was still closer to being a frog; still no more the talker than I was the subdued one. I began to blame myself. Did I not bring up subjects of interest? What kind of woman had he dated before? I knew less about him than I knew about the guys I worked with at the automotive plant. Frustrated, puzzled, and yes, more than a little annoyed, I knew that I would have to stop seeing him.

One Saturday evening as he walked me to the door, he asked me out for the following Monday night. Instead of causing a scene, I decided to be kind. I told him that I had to go out of town with my sister. I was ashamed of myself for lying, but whatever Clay's problem was, I couldn't make it mine. I let him down as gently as I could. Then, without skipping a beat, he asked me out for the following Friday night. I told him to call me on Thursday and we'd decide then. The yellow streak down my back had shown itself once again.

I had endured an entire month of dating this man and he hadn't told me much about himself, hadn't fully answered my questions about his love life, nor had he held my hand or kissed me goodnight. Was he gay? Did he have problems with intimacy? Oh my goodness—was he secretly married? My mind jumped from one nutty thought to the other as I tried to figure out the inner workings of this odd man. Couples with a genuine connection, soul mates as I like to call them, are happy with few words between them on occasion. But in a new relationship, with that small window of opportunity a couple has to really get to know one another, silence is not golden. It's just weird.

What was wrong with him could no longer matter to me. I knew I couldn't work forty hours a week and then labor overtime at simple conversation. Saturday night should be fun-filled, exciting and romantic; a quiet evening with talk of travel, dreams and life over candlelight and dinner. No candles at Ponderosa Steak House—the only place we ever went!

Clay's call came in like clockwork that Thursday evening. I didn't want to answer the phone but I knew I had to if I was going to move on with my life. I didn't waste any time telling him that while I was away, I had time to think and felt we needed to take a break from each other. I told him that it was obvious that we were different people going in opposite directions in our lives and I needed to get back to my normal routine. He told me he was disappointed and he urged me to call him if ever I wanted to pick up where we left off. I was so relieved when I hung up the phone. It's my nature to try to figure out what makes people tick, but one hour with Clay Hutchison was simply too much heavy lifting.

Looking back, these boring dates would be a cakewalk compared to what I would endure in the future. Who knew that the biggest problems of my life would begin with another simple telephone call?

Who ARE you?

Exactly one year to the day of our first date, my phone rang again as I was curled up on the couch watching an old Kate Hepburn movie. It was Clay. I couldn't believe it. What this man lacked in conversational skills he certainly made up for in tenacity. They say time makes bad memories fade and that must have been the case for me when I said "Yes" to his request to take me to dinner, and *this* time, wonder of wonders, a movie on Saturday night. I was prepared to spend the entire date mentally balancing my checkbook and looking at my watch, but I was pleasantly surprised and a bit bewildered by his complete personality change that evening. What a difference a year had made in this man! I felt myself wanting to ask "Who are you and what have you done with Clay?" No doubt my reaction was due to watching "Invasion of the Body Snatchers" on the late show as a child.

From the moment Clay pulled in to the driveway—this time with a shiny new pickup truck—he actually held up his end of the conversation and then some. As we talked of family, living in a small town, life and work after our school years and the like, I began to see that perhaps Clay had been reluctant to talk with me before, due to a particularly embarrassing dating history. He had never dated. As in... *ever.*

I had enjoyed my share of beaus and had turned down a couple of marriage proposals. I figured any normal man his age would have gone through dozens of women and a few marriages by now. When he told me his secret, I was floored. Mr. Hutchison's first foray into the dating world was at age 42 with *me*—a woman he had "crushed on" when she was still in Bobbie socks. He told me he had never met a woman he cared about enough to date and that he was so busy with his farm and taking care of his elderly father that going out with women simply had not been a priority. His explanation and his reasoning seemed palatable so I didn't question him any further about it.

Looking back, I have one question for myself: What was *I* smokin'?

For the next few weeks, I was actually looking forward to our Saturday night outings to—where else?—Ponderosa Steak House in Lebanon. Like that onion the psychologists enjoy talking about, this man carefully revealed layer after layer of one precious personality gem after another as each date progressed. I felt like an explorer who had wandered onto a remote island paradise. Where had *this* Clay been all my life? Technically, he had existed about an hour and a half to the north in a small Kentucky town.

The Virgin Boy

In my romantic teenage fantasies, I would meet this strong, handsome southern gentleman who only had eyes for me—a man who had been looking for the perfect girl all his life and would not rest until he discovered his Rose in tiny Lafayette, Tennessee. I was looking for my leading man—the man who would slay dragons and make the boogeyman go away. Could Clay be the one? He seemed so manly—so protective.

He was a real gentleman. Could this really be happening to *me*? Has this leading man saved himself and pined after me and only me all these years? He told me he knew I was the only woman for him the minute he laid eyes on me at the Fountain Run party. This was the stuff my romantic novels were made of.

In those first few weeks of our third chance together, Clay shared with me his fears about our first date the year before, and how nervous he was as he pulled into my driveway that evening. He also tried to explain away his behavior that awful month of our initial courtship. Apparently, he felt he was at a disadvantage in the situation since it was his first experience with entertaining a lady. I was beginning to understand and even empathize.

By the third month, Clay seemed to be getting his sea legs with the whole dating scene. He walked me to the door one evening and planted the most exquisite kiss on my lips—a far more passionate kiss than I remembered during our first meeting at Fountain Run. A more tender and loving kiss than I can remember receiving from any man in my entire life.

The next Saturday night following one of those fabulous front door kisses, I whispered "I love you" before I could stop myself. It just slipped out and there was nothing I could do to change it.

Quickly, as if being pursued by a large bear, Clay flew off the front porch.

"I'll call you about next weekend," he said, as he jumped in his truck like a shot, squealing tires to get out of the driveway. When I slammed the front door behind me, I was wishing I had slammed my head in there as well. How could I have shown my cards so soon?

You dummy! You never want to be the first to say that to a man—especially a man who moves at a glacial pace like Clay! Well, what's done is done. If I never see him again, lesson learned. All these things were going through my mind as I readied for bed. I'd have all day tomorrow to regret what I just did. No point in losing sleep over it tonight.

The next day at work I couldn't get my mind off Clay. Everywhere I looked I saw his face. I wore a permanent smile and my co-workers were asking why I was so happy. I was in love and it was written all over my face. So what if I had told him that I loved him? He'll just have to deal with it. If he can't stand the idea of a woman being in love with him, then I don't need him anyway.

Oh, but I *did* need him. He was too good to be true. He was everything I had ever hoped for in a man. A man of appropriate age with no children, no ex-wives, no alimony payments and most importantly—no *baggage* that required a one-hundred-dollars-an-hour shrink.

Or so I thought at the time.

A Good Sign

I took it as a good sign when Clay called me from a pay phone around noon the following Saturday and asked me if he could come by for a few minutes since he had something to show me. I was working in the flowers outside and was covered in potting soil from head to toe when Mama called me to the phone. I had only a few minutes to jump in the shower and put on clean clothes before a bright red, shiny, new convertible pulled up in the driveway. It was Clay and he looked absolutely grand.

"Well, what do you think?" He had just bought the car in Goodlettsville.

"I love it, but where's the truck?"

"That gas-guzzler is at home. This is to burn up the road between Kentucky and Tennessee sweet Rosie!" He figured that we could go to Nashville and back on one dollar's worth of gasoline in that car and that it was worth every penny just from the gas it saved. That's my thrifty Clay.

At that moment, I knew that I was overthinking my little "I love you" slip-up. I didn't give it another thought and I vowed to say and do whatever came naturally from that day forward. Apparently, Clay adopted this same attitude.

That night we took the new convertible to Barron River Reservoir and parked in the perfect spot. With the bright stars and full moon reflecting on the water, Clay told me that he loved me.

We made out like teenagers and at long last, consummated our love and christened the new car. It was quite obviously Clay's first sexual experience.

Later that decade......

I would *like* to say that our relationship moved forward at the speed of a Lifetime cable movie. I would *like* to say that within six months, Clay and I got married and were having our honeymoon dinner at Ponderosa Steaks in Gatlinburg. I would like to say that ten years later we were getting kids off to school, saving up for braces and college, and planning family picnics and vacations. But I can't say any of that.

Ten years and four months went by before Clay Hutchison surprised me over dinner and asked me to marry him. In a decade of dating this man, I had not met his family, had not seen his farm nor had I seen the town where he grew up. We had never discussed living arrangements, children, housing, finances, or any of the things normal couples who look toward marriage talk about during their courtship. Now that we were engaged, Clay wanted us to do all of this at the speed of light.

After he popped the question at dinner, we drove to our spot at Barron River Reservoir for old time's sake. The next afternoon, we spent a fun day in Tompkinsville where Clay bought me the most beautiful engagement ring at the jewelers. We shared a celebratory lunch at a quaint little diner on the square and then drove to Clay's farm, eager to share our good news with his family. I was so excited—and a bit nervous—about being in his home for the first time.

Clay had told me so much about it, but it never seemed as though there was a good opportunity to go up there, since his elderly father was living with him. He didn't volunteer very much information about his family, except to discuss their duties on the farm or small talk about something funny that happened at the stock sale.

The Hutchison Compound

The Hutchison family shared their lives on a working farm that started out with less than seventy acres when Clay's mother and father, Bernard and Ramona, married and inherited the home place from Bernard Hutchison Sr. and his wife, Sara. As the years progressed and the little ones were born, the couple built a large ranch-style house just a few yards from the two-bedroom cottage that was original to the farm. Clay's sister and brother-in-law now lived in that tiny cottage. Less than two acres away, Clay's brother and his wife built a new log home. The Hutchison Compound, as it's called by the neighbors, is expansive and belongs on the cover of Progressive Farmer magazine. Clay has seen to that.

Every dollar he made in cattle from the time he was twelve, went back in to the farm. As land became available adjacent to the Hutchison farm, Clay would buy a few acres at a time, deeded in his name, until the farm became a whopping 650 acres of Kentucky Bluegrass with more than 700 head of Black Angus cattle roaming as far as the eye can see.

The 52-year-old Clay had always lived here with his parents, sleeping in the same room he had slept in as a boy, hanging his toothbrush in the stand next to his father's denture cream as the years passed.

After the untimely death of his mother, Clay felt an obligation to stay there to give his lonely dad what comfort he could. That was my Clay. He was so thoughtful of his family. How could I not love a man like that? I didn't think a thing about it when he told me over lunch that we would be moving my things into the ranch house with him and his dad after we married. He told me that there was plenty of room and with his father's health failing, the old guy couldn't be left alone in that big house.

I was on board and enthusiastic. I loved Clay. Wherever thou goest I will go… and all that stuff a woman thinks when she's in love.

The Pits

I've always been outgoing and ready to meet new people, but walking into that ranch house for the first time after our engagement, I felt as though I was walking into a lion's den. Just as Clay had been painfully quiet, making me squirm on our first date, his relatives were sitting in uncomfortable silence as we entered the living room. It was like the waiting room at the doctor's office. Now, there was no question. My groom-to-be had come by his low-key personality honestly.

We had only been there a few minutes when Clay asked his sister, Rena, if she had seen my ring. She didn't bother looking up from her needlepoint to dryly quip "I saw it." (She had not). This bunch reminded me of the Culhanes on the old Nashville comedy show *Hee-Haw* as they sat elbow to elbow on the long sofa. Only the tick of the antique clock in the hall kept me from thinking I had gone deaf. I took a seat in the wing chair, facing the sofa, near the desk across the large room. Clay sat at the other side of the room in a recliner.

There was Clay's dad, 81-year-old Bernard, who had what appeared to be a permanent frown on his ruddy and deeply wrinkled face. A long swath of wispy silver hair was combed over his entire head from a long part over the right ear. I shuddered to think how that 'do' must behave in a wind storm. His glasses were thick and magnified his pale blue eyes—eyes like Clay's. He wore a neat, clean flannel shirt tucked in to clean, crisply ironed jeans.

His work boots, obviously retired from years on the farm, were well worn but clean, his brown work socks stopping short to expose an inch of skinny, lily-white, hairless shin as he sat on the couch with his legs crossed. His hands were calloused and it appeared he had signs of dark grease under his fingernails. A walking cane was propped on the couch beside him. His bum leg was the result of an ornery bull trying to run him over in a barn stall a few years back.

Clay had certainly gotten his looks from his mother, as I could tell from her photographs on the mantle. I'm sure little brother's great build and good looks were not lost on the older, less attractive siblings and their mates.

Sitting next to Bernard was Clay's fifty-four-year-old brother, Thomas, who had an unfortunate chipped front tooth and a bulbous, almost purple nose. His thick brown mustache and big black glasses gave him the appearance of someone in a clever disguise. His wife, Elsa, was very proper in her watercolor-flowered silk dress and she sat bent slightly forward with her hands clasped across her knees as if to announce that her job was to give me the once-over. Her salt and pepper hair was swept up in a tight bun and revealed a graceful long neck which she had highlighted with a single strand of pearls. She was intimidating and in her younger days was probably very attractive. Her translucent, white skin and green, darting eyes were striking among this divan full of people who didn't look as though they even enjoyed each other's company much less wanted to be awake for this 'welcome to the family' party.

Sitting beside the shy and withdrawn Rena, who still had her head buried in her needlepoint, it was patently obvious that, unlike her sister-in-law, Elsa had been brought up with the proper social graces. At least she asked a few polite questions to break the silence. Elsa was a school teacher and looked every inch a confident, well-heeled, disciplinarian.

Rena, like her father, was thin and gaunt and looked as though few smiles had visited her face. There were no telltale laugh lines, although deep vertical wrinkles around her mouth indicated a lifetime of sneaking a puff of a cigarette or two. Her graying hair was tinted a pale blonde and she had it in a stylish bob. She had bitten her nails down to the nub, but her fingers were talented and nimble as she pulled the wool thread through the fabric to make the pattern of a beautiful sunflower on a pillow top. Rena was a cooking, sewing, hearth-minding homemaker and she ran her home on the family compound like a drill sergeant, according to Clay. Everything was in place and her days on the farm were organized with military precision. The only sound she had made so far on this afternoon was to fib about seeing my ring.

Rena's husband, Therlow, took up the remaining room on the sofa. Only 5'2 and weighing in at around 290 pounds, he wore his insecurities on his tattered sleeve and his dirty, red, Pioneer Seed Corn baseball cap on the back of his large head with the bill curled up in a tight little circle. Worn in that manner, it had done little to protect his large, freckled face from the sun and his skin was dark red and leathery as a result. He had a yellow/gray Van Dyke beard and felt no need to lose the plug of chewing tobacco stuffed tightly in his jaw before sitting in the parlor to meet his brother-in-law's fiancée. His faded, plaid flannel shirt was barely holding on to its strained buttons and had worked its way out of his jeans which, by this time, had slipped well below his large, melon-shaped midsection. His country drawl was almost unintelligible.

Yep. No doubt about it. All in all, I had gotten the pick of this litter in the looks department with my gorgeous fiancé, but I had my work cut out for me if I was expected to keep a running commentary going in this household. I felt as if a time machine had jetted me back to my first, boring date with Clay.

I answered the few questions Elsa had for me with enthusiasm and even threw in some extra information, but for the most part, I felt all my answers hit the ground with a thud. Where had I worked? In a café and a couple of factories. Where did I live? In Lafayette with my widowed Mama. Where did I go to college? I didn't. Clay rescued me by chiming in with comments about the farm and how the heifers needed to be turned in to the other pasture by tomorrow. That got the men talking. Even Rena and Elsa had opinions about who should be hired to repair the barn roof and how many workers should be brought in to help with the final hay cutting of the season.

Now that I was off the hot seat, I had a quiet moment to observe my new family-to-be as they were enthralled in conversation. Occasionally, Therlow would pick up his coffee can and spit into it before offering his opinion, but that disgusting habit aside, this family looked like any family you would see anywhere...on another planet.

This was Americana. This was going to be my new family, my next Christmas morning—the people seated at the table for my next Thanksgiving meal. Crammed onto this brown and harvest gold Herculon sofa next to the wagon wheel coffee table and threadbare recliner, were the people with whom I would have to share my wonderful Clay. The man who had loved me since I was a teenager, was now showing off his future bride to the people he cared about most.

I was his first girlfriend and his first sexual experience when he was a spry 42. He was my world and I was his. Now, ten years later, I was going to be his wife and helpmate here on the farm that was part of him, here with the people that were his family. This is the way I've always heard it should be. I couldn't wait until Clay was my husband.

It was the following weekend when Clay told me that some members of his family were begging him to get a prenuptial agreement. He said he told them that I loved him and was marrying him for that reason and nothing else. We didn't have any kind of agreement between us the day we married but I would have signed one if Clay had asked me to. I didn't know what any of those discussions with his family entailed and I didn't want to know. I felt that was Clay's business. I had a modest nest-egg put aside for a rainy day. I figured I didn't need the money Clay made from his cattle business anyway and I intended to pull my own weight by continuing my job at the factory. It wasn't as though I was marrying into the Rockefeller family. Why was such a big deal being made over this? I would have the answer to my question many years later.

Pappy Ain't Invited

Forty-two-year-old brides-to-be react differently than those girls in their twenties who are engaged to be married. For me, planning my little wedding took on a more pragmatic tone and every detail—down to the guest list—was discussed without emotion and without drama. Clay didn't hesitate to tell me he didn't want *any* of his family at our wedding. My antenna should have gone up at that moment, but that big clue whizzed right past my head and into the pink clouds of joy that were swirling around in my mature brain. A young bride would have thrown a fit if her groom had made such a statement. She would have, at the very least, tried to get to the bottom of why her man abhorred his own family to the point of exclusion from this big day. I just let it go, perhaps thinking at the time that it was none of my business and that families go through these phases. Then again, maybe I wasn't thinking at all.

The Big Day

With only a few girls from work invited, in addition to all of my family, the guest list was very small. The wedding was in the living room of my cottage which I decorated with a few roses and candles from the flower shop on the square. My three nieces were bridesmaids and looked simply beautiful in the dresses my sister made especially for their Auntie Rose's wedding.

I found my dress of candlelight cream silk at a thrift shop and paid ten dollars for it. I was so proud! I wore flowers in my hair and carried a bouquet of pink roses—my favorite. As the guests stood around the tiny room, we exchanged our vows and afterwards we all went in to the dining room for cake and fruit punch. One of my friends from work, whose hobby was photography, took some fabulous wedding photos that I still cherish.

My brothers stood up with Clay during the ceremony and couldn't resist the urge to act as most groomsmen do, writing on Clay's red convertible in white shoe polish, "Just Married… Finally." We honeymooned in a little motel not far from Barron River—the scene of our first love making session.

Clay was so nervous and excited that he left his keys in the car door overnight and didn't notice until the next morning when we turned the room upside down looking them. It didn't matter. Nothing mattered. We were so happy. I figured we could tell our grandkids about our antics someday.

Home at Last

The next morning, Clay carried me over the threshold of his beautiful farmhouse, nestled high atop a hill in one of the most picturesque areas of Kentucky I have ever visited. I could easily understand why this farm was such a part of him. He didn't share a lot, but when he did talk, I could always see the excitement in his eyes when he related something that had happened on the farm that week. It was his favorite subject and I was thrilled that he could get so excited about his daily work after so many years. I had waited all my life, but I finally found a man who loved his home, loved his life and most importantly, loved me for ME. I was the perfect life mate for him. I was frugal, not afraid to get my hands dirty, and knew a lot about the country life. What a team we were going to be!

Clay was a man of few words, but I felt that he spoke from the heart. We were two mature, level-headed people who pursued our dreams and met our challenges, and at last, we had found our way to each other. Ten years of dating certainly peeled away many complicated layers of this onion and I had yet to shed one single tear in the process. But that was about to change.

Life With Father

Clay's dad Bernard had farmed all his life and, as a certified accountant, prepared tax returns for people in the community. He continued to help his son manage the farm and make major decisions concerning the Angus cattle they raised, but his health and his bum leg didn't allow him to get out and do much of the physical work that farming required. In the spring, the old fellow would climb aboard the giant tractor and disk a spot for the compound's vegetable garden but for the most part, he made sure the feed was delivered, the books were kept, workers hired for various projects and the machinery repaired, clean, and ready to go.

Not many new brides would be keen on moving in with her new husband and his elderly dad but that's what I did and I didn't think it odd at the time. In fact, before I learned much about Bernard, I felt sorry for the old guy and was glad I would be there to keep the house neat, the meals cooked, and clothes clean and pressed for the father of this wonderful man I married. Bernard's room in the east wing of the house remained closed and locked at all times and I was concerned that I wouldn't be allowed in there to dust and run the vacuum, but Clay told me not to worry about it.

Shortly after I moved in, Clay finally told me the tragic story of his mother. I had always been curious as to how she died, but I didn't want to stir up painful memories. Clay hadn't talked of her very much and managed to change the subject whenever I mentioned her name. I took that as a sign that there must have been something inherently painful surrounding her death when she was in her early fifties.

Ramona Martin was a blue blood—the daughter of a former Illinois senator whose family was in the oil business. She majored in public policy at the University of Kentucky with plans to follow in her father's footsteps and enter public service, but a party following a victorious basketball game her sophomore year changed all that. A friend introduced this tall, willow-y brunette to accounting major, Bernard Hutchison. The two fell in love and against her parent's wishes, young Ramona dropped out of college to marry her man and follow him to his small cattle farm so far away from everything she knew. She came in to the marriage with a hefty dowry and a brilliant mind for business, but Bernard refused to allow her to work outside the home. It wasn't long before the newlyweds were able to build and furnish their dream house—mostly with Ramona's money—beside the cottage of Bernard's parents on the farm.

According to Clay, Ramona insisted upon keeping her money, investments, checking and savings separate from Bernard's, and her independence spawned many heated arguments in the marriage. Clay said he thought his late Grandpa Martin in Chicago had strings attached to that money since the entire Martin family was against the marriage from the beginning.

College for the kids, books, clothing, and Christmas presents, all came from Ramona's checking account. The children never wanted for anything even when the cattle and tobacco markets took hits. No doubt, Ramona's financial independence emasculated the boorish and chauvinistic Bernard, sending him around the bend.

Clay said he thought it was a good idea for a wife to have her own 'mad money' and he encouraged me to keep my separate bank account in Lafayette after we married if I wished.

Dad's Dark Side

With all of Ramona's resources, however, Clay said that his mother never seemed happy. It made Clay uncomfortable to hear his dad make unkind remarks about his mother behind her back and it upset him when they got into heated arguments right in front of him. Clay said when he was very young, he remembers his mother would hold him in her arms and cry for no reason as she rocked him to sleep. He said he tried his best to comfort her, but he always felt so inadequate. Talking to his dad about the pain he was inflicting on both of them was out of the question. Bernard lashed out at Clay by saying nothing could be done for a clueless fool who brings these things upon herself. Little Clay felt helpless when it came to mending his mother's broken heart. My sweet husband had grown up with traditional roles reversed—his childhood spent as caretaker of a broken woman. I wondered how that affected his psyche now that he was a man.

As I listened to Clay talk about his troubled mother, I couldn't help but wonder—why did a woman who had so much going for her choose to stay with a cruel, emotionally abusive man like Bernard? His shabby treatment of her surely didn't begin suddenly when the children were born. I would be out of that marriage so quickly it would make my abusive spouse's hair change color. I wouldn't have allowed my children to observe this! Why, oh why didn't Ramona leave?

The Family Tragedy

In the late 1970's, Ramona was in the rose garden teaching her 6 year old granddaughter to ride a bike while the parents, Clay's brother, Thomas and his wife, Elsa, attended a wedding. When Mrs. Hutchison stepped inside to answer a telephone call from Bernard, the child rode her bicycle outside the safety of the garden gate, down the hill, and into the path of a truck. She was killed instantly.

The distraught Mrs. Hutchison blamed herself for her only grandchild's death and slipped into a deep depression. She began to drink brandy during the day—lots of it—and became a recluse. I found out later that her depression and isolation were compounded by Bernard who continuously reminded her that she had been careless on that day and that she indeed was the reason her granddaughter was dead. Clay overheard Bernard tell Ramona that "every time Thomas and Elsa looked at her ugly face they were reminded why they no longer had a child." A few months later, Mrs. Hutchison took an overdose of her heart medication, downed it with half a bottle of brandy, and died in her sleep.

Incredibly, I learned from the old man himself these dark details about his role in driving this poor woman to an early grave. I was dusting the library table one morning and when I moved the photograph of Mrs. Hutchison, Bernard began telling me the story from his skewed point of view. He bragged about how he was the one to constantly hound "the old woman" as he referred to her, about her many shortcomings, claiming that he always knew her "stupidity" would result in a terrible accident someday.

He proudly wore the contempt for his dead wife as if it were a badge of honor. His harsh words contributed to her suicide. He knew it and he didn't give a flip. Only one thing he said that afternoon made any sense. He said that his wife was "better off."

Truer words have never been spoken. Given the choice of being married to this miserable cretin or dying, I would have put a gun in my mouth without a second thought. Pills wouldn't work quickly enough but then again, there wouldn't have been enough liquor in the world to get me to marry him in the first place.

I found Bernard's brash, boorish attitude repulsive and I avoided conversations with him from that day forward. We would go months at a time without saying one word to each other. I continued to work the second shift at Carter's Automotive which meant I was stuck in that house with him until around two in the afternoon. Avoiding him wasn't easy, but in order to keep my peace of mind, I had to stay out of his way.

How my sweet and thoughtful Clay could have come from the loins of this character was beyond me.

The Newlyweds

Life with Clay for the next few years was upbeat and always active. Saturday mornings meant hopping on the 4-wheelers, going on picnics by the lake, picking wildflowers, and riding the fencerow on horseback to check for repairs that would be needed in the week to come.

Clay still wasn't the most talkative man I'd ever met but I could live forever off those few beautiful words he uttered regularly: "I love you, Rosie!" He would pick the most unexpected times to pay compliments. My hair would be in a ponytail and my face covered in dirt after a day of gardening and he would look at me, smile, and say, "Rose, you are the most beautiful woman I've ever known."

My heart was so full and my life had changed so much since this sweet, gentle man had mustered the courage to call me on that spring night more than a decade ago. If our romance was still this strong after so many years, I couldn't wait to see what our twentieth anniversary would bring!

I woke before dawn each morning with a smile to prepare a hearty breakfast for my husband. Hot biscuits, scrambled eggs, country ham, gravy, hash-browned potatoes, fruit salad, and fresh-squeezed orange juice were among his breakfast favorites. Clay got up around five to jog his usual four miles. Afterwards, I brought his coffee while he shaved and got ready for his day. He never failed to come to the table looking as handsome as the day we met.

We would have a few quiet moments together before Bernard woke up and came sauntering in with his disheveled comb-over, three-day beard and ragged house coat. Without a word, except to bark out his breakfast order to me, Bernard would sit down and attempt to make as much noise as he could—apparently trying to cough up a lung—just to make his presence known. Clay and I would look at each other and smile.

The factory was a little over an hour's drive away for me now that I had moved north, but my shift didn't begin until 3PM, so after Clay climbed aboard the tractor to begin his farming each morning, I'd go back to bed and catch a few more winks to energize myself for the long night of widget-watching to come. The extra nap time not only offered much needed rest, but gave me the space I needed from old man Hutchison. Thank God he lived at the other end of this long, meandering ranch-style house. The less I saw of him the better.

The Family Messenger

One morning after sending Clay off to the stock sale, I stayed up to clean the kitchen and get a few small ironing chores out of the way. I set up the ironing board in front of the bay window in the kitchen to enjoy the morning sun and to watch the finches enjoy the seed I religiously supplied in the feeder.

It wasn't long before old man Hutchison shuffled past. I watched his reflection in the window as he poured a cup of coffee and casually lit one of his unfiltered Camels.

"You know, no one in this family wants you here." He delivered the line matter-of-factly as he blew the smoke from his hairy nostrils. For a moment, I thought the old fart was either developing a sense of humor or perhaps, Alzheimer's.

"Excuse me?" I turned and looked straight at him, which was not an easy task, considering how he looked at that hour of the morning.

"Let me spell it out for you, dingbat, just in case you're as stupid as the bitch I was married to," he continued with his vitriolic spew. "You are not wanted here. Clay's brother and sister have been through enough in their lives. They want you gone. Dead. Outta here. You're an unwelcomed stranger in our family and you always will be." With that, he crushed his cigarette on the stack of clean plates I had just taken from the dishwasher.

"Hell, for that matter," he continued with a smirk, "I'm sick of lookin' at your ugly face around here every day!"

Without taking my eyes off my ironing, I said the only thing I could say with a walnut-sized lump in my throat and tears streaming down my face.

"Clay wants me here—that's all that matters!"

The old man seized the perfect opportunity to plant a seed. "I wouldn't be so cock-sure about that if I were you. He's got other women. And I wouldn't be so quick to run to Clay about our little discussion. That'll backfire if you're not careful! If my son knew you were causing me trouble he'd dump you like the trash you are! His allegiance is to his family, and trash like you *ain't* family!"

That morning was the first of what became a sad routine for this crusty old man with the nasty attitude and tobacco-stained teeth. Where Clay's words were sweet, soothing and light, his father's words became more hate-filled, frightening and dark with each passing day. He would pass me in the hall—sometimes with Clay only a few feet away in the den—and would whisper the words "Idiot," or "Dingbat," or, his all-time favorite go-to word, "whore."

One afternoon, I arrived home from the market and began to unload bag after bag of groceries—climbing the steps to the kitchen from the garage and across the giant room to place the bags on the countertops. Bernard sat at the table smoking his cigarette, never offering to hold the door for me. As I made my way with the final load, my vision almost blocked by the full bags, Bernard bent over from his chair and stuck his walking cane in my path. My legs tangled, the bags slipped from my arms, and down I went. I laid there for just a moment, the breath knocked out of me, my arm bruised and bleeding.

"You clumsy idiot," he said, and he dropped his smoldering cigarette directly in front of my face as I lay on the floor. He laughed and crushed out the butt with his boot. That night, Bernard shared his twist on the incident as dinner table conversation. He suggested to Clay that the door jamb needed repair because my rubber-soled shoes caught it and I had tripped while bringing in the groceries. He added, while giving me a slight grin, "Our sweet Rose could have been seriously hurt, son!"

Of all the hateful remarks that the old man decided were his duty to impart in Clay's absence, none affected me as much as when he chose the morning of my birthday to spew "Why don't you leave? Why don't you die, you insect? Why were you ever born? You're just in everybody's way!" I don't know why that particular rant had such impact on me, but it did.

I took it with me to work that day. It rang in my ears and before I could get a grip, the tears began to flow and I had to run to the restroom to gather myself.

That evening when I got home to Clay, I tried to put on a brave face and pretend that nothing was wrong. At bedtime, I kissed him goodnight and told him I was going to read for a while and wind down from the hectic day. What I really wanted to do was run down to the barn and scream—scream and cry until I couldn't cry anymore. I felt as if I had an elephant sitting on my chest and I couldn't breathe.

How could I tell this beautiful man who was so good to me that his father was a cruel, evil, devil? What if he didn't believe me as the old man had warned? I found myself trying to psycho-analyze the entire Hutchison family, member-by-member. Did old man Hutchison emotionally abuse Clay in the same way he abused his wife? Is this why my darling husband is so withdrawn? Is this why he was so shy and timid when we first met? Is this why Rena allows her mental-midget husband to run her life and talk down to her?

My heart broke at the thought as I looked on the wall at Clay's precious baby portrait. My sweet little Clay. What have you endured with this horrible man? How did poor Mrs. Hutchison last as long as she did? She was certainly stronger than I, because I can't continue to live like this.

I sobbed uncontrollably as I sat in the study located in the middle of this long house. I was trying to be quiet but suddenly, I felt a hand on my shoulder. I froze. For one awful moment, I feared it might be the old man.

Maybe he had thought of the perfect combination of horrid words—just the right threats that might take me over the edge and send me the way of the late Mrs. Hutchison. I'm sure the old man was hoping that I would someday ingest enough pills to put myself out of his way permanently. Maybe he had some ideas of his own for my demise.

"Honey, what's wrong?" Thank God it was my sweet husband who was now kneeling beside me and stroking my hair.

"Is everything alright with us, my love? Why are you crying?" Clay pulled me toward him with a warm embrace.

"Oh, sweetheart, everything's fine with us, of course." I sat up to wipe the smeared mascara from beneath my eyes. "We're fine. Someone else has hurt my feelings." I couldn't stop the heaving in my chest.

"Who has hurt you, love?" Clay asked as he wiped a tear from my cheek.

I paused and thought for a moment about what the old man had said. Bernard warned that Clay wouldn't believe me. He said that Clay's allegiance was to him and not to me. No matter. I couldn't keep this inside any longer. I had to tell Clay everything. He's my husband. I owed him an explanation.

"Your father has been telling me for the past few months that no one wants me here, and that everyone in the family wishes I were dead," I whispered between sobs, terrified that any moment Bernard would walk in. Surprisingly, Clay didn't seem shocked in the least to hear this. His expression didn't change as he listened, still holding me and stroking my hair.

I told him everything and I didn't spare the details—about the nasty name calling, and Bernard's hearty laughter after tripping me in the kitchen with his cane. The whole, awful, sick story spilled out of me. I felt as though I had just vomited. It was such a relief to get it out in the open.

"Did you tell him that *I* wanted you here and that's all that matters?" Clay was calm and cool as if he had heard this before—indeed—because he had heard it before. He grew up hearing these same details from his poor mother every day of his life. Like Ramona, I was crying late in the night and Clay was trying to comfort me.

"Yes, I told him that you wanted me here but that won't stop him. He's relentless! This has been going on for months," I cried. "He's telling me that you won't believe any of this and that you have other women and don't need me anymore."

"I'll talk to him first thing in the morning." Clay assured me. "You sleep late and don't worry about breakfast. I'll take care of everything. Is that okay my love?" Clay hugged me and went to the kitchen for a glass of water. As I collected myself, I felt light as a feather. This heavy burden had been lifted. My knight in shining armor was indeed going to slay this dragon in the kitchen the following morning. Or at least, that's how I pictured the scene going down. Done and done. Who knew it was going to be that simple?

I should have known that Clay would believe me. I should have told him weeks ago and saved myself all this angst. I've been trying to deal with the old man's abuse alone when I didn't have to. I felt so silly for doubting my beloved. I had secretly hoped that Clay would be uncontrollably furious once he heard what Bernard had been doing, but then again, who knows the mindset of a man who has spent his entire life cleaning up the messes of his horrible old coot of a father?

    I was almost too mad at myself to relax. Why had I suffered in silence for so long? Why had I believed the old man when he said that Clay would take his side? In spite of my self-loathing at all that had transpired, the emotions of the previous months had left me ready to crash. I had the best sleep I had enjoyed in weeks that night, thanks to the promises of this precious man who loved me so much.

Chilly Mornings

Whatever Clay said to his father certainly must have done the trick because the next morning, old man Hutchison was furious.

"You're gonna wish you had never crossed me," he warned as I came into the kitchen. I looked past him as though he didn't exist. For the next few weeks, it was pretty chilly around the house after Clay left to go to work. The old man ignored me and I was fine with that. I kept busy and stayed out of his way until time to go to work every afternoon. If I had to iron, I set up the board in our bedroom. I got as much of the housework and laundry out of the way as I could before breakfast and then slept until time for work just to avoid Bernard.

Exactly two months later, as if on some kind of sick schedule, the abuse started again. This time, old man Hutchison took it up a notch.

Early one morning, I kissed Clay goodbye and he was off to the Farmer's Co-op to buy a new hay roller. The old man was back in the study on the phone trying to line up a crew to do some fencing down in the lower pasture. As long as he had something to do and stayed away from me and the kitchen, I could enjoy my mornings and have a normal life before heading to work.

I was mixing up some muffins to leave for Clay's dessert when Bernard pegged in to pour himself some coffee. At least I thought that's what he had on his mind.

Just as I bent over to place the pan in the oven, I heard his walking cane hit the floor and felt two hands cup my breasts. Bernard pulled me into his crotch and began to grind against me. I screamed, grabbed the crusty old hands with the black greasy nails and had to stop myself from kicking him in the groin—my first inclination after taking a self-defense class at work.

"What the hell are you doing? Are you drunk?" I screamed and slapped him in the face as hard as I could manage. Angry tears welled in my eyes.

Bernard began to laugh so hard that he got into a coughing fit and fell against the kitchen cabinet. I was hoping he would choke to death. "You liked that. You were askin' for it," he said, his face red from the dry hacking.

"Keep your hands off me you…dirty old…bastard! You've messed with the wrong woman for the last time! Ramona had to take your crap but I don't have to. I'm telling Clay!"

With that threat, he picked up the kitchen phone and launched into a rant.

"Here! Call the Co-op and ask for Clay. Tell him right now what happened. Let me know how that works out for you, bitch! He'll never believe you instead of me. We don't trust lying-ass women around here! Damn, I wish you would just freakin' die! But, you go ahead and tell Clay what I did. He'll throw you out on your gold-diggin' ear! Why do you think he was in his forties and still single when you met him, stupid?"

As I ran out of the kitchen sobbing, he screamed behind me: "I've felt better tits on an old sow anyway!" He continued to cough and laugh until I was so far down the hall I couldn't hear him anymore. I ran into the bedroom and locked the door behind me, fearing that any moment now my abuser would try to assault me again. Or worse.

What now? How do I reach Clay? I've got to tell him this instant because this must be dealt with immediately. This cannot wait until I return from work this evening. What if the old man gets to Clay and makes up an outlandish tale before I can tell him what happened? My mind was reeling and Bernard's awful words were ringing in my ears as I lay on the bed. I couldn't call in sick to work because that would mean staying home with this twisted bastard, but certainly I didn't feel like facing anyone today. I could drive to the Co-op and meet Clay there. How do I handle this?

I heard the old man walk down the hall to his room and slam the door. After what seemed like an eternity, I heard the pick-up truck start and Bernard was headed down the driveway. Was he going to intercept Clay and offer up a crazy story?

I couldn't think about that now. He was gone. I was finally alone. Only when I saw the truck disappear over the hill down on the highway did I feel safe enough to get in the shower to wash the events of this horrible morning off my crawling skin.

When Clay got home with the new hay roller, I was waiting for him in my car. I ran to his arms sobbing and he thought that someone in my family had died. As we walked back into the house, I gave him every detail of the morning's events—what Bernard did, what he said. I even re-enacted how Bernard grabbed me as Clay sat at the kitchen table, stone-faced.

"Honey, I think we need to call the doctor, okay?" he said, after hearing me out.

"I'm so glad to hear you say that, Clay. He needs to be checked out. He might be in the first stages of Alzheimer's with these fits of rage and this inappropriate behavior."

"I wasn't talking about Daddy, sweetheart. You need to see a counselor or a psychiatrist to sort through all this."

I couldn't believe what my husband was saying. His father acts like an abusive pervert and he thinks *I'M* the one who needs to see a shrink. This made no sense at all.

"Clay, yes, I agree, I'm going to need someone to help me get over this horrible abuse I've been putting up with from your father, but HE needs to either be medically treated or punished for what he has done to me!" I was raising my voice to my husband for the first time in our marriage.

"We'll call Dr. Stewart in the morning. He was mom's doctor and he's great. I'll go with you," Clay said, still not offering to do anything about the offending party.

"I'm sure your mom's doctor has already heard an earful about your disgusting father!" I cried as I stormed out and headed to work. I had already called my supervisor and told her I would be an hour late and she was sweet and understanding; telling me to take all the time I needed. I was treated like gold by the people I worked with. They knew they could depend on me to work overtime, to train new people, or to meet the owners and give them a tour of the assembly line and I wouldn't complain. How sad that today, I looked forward to clocking-in more than I relished clocking-out of the factory. I was dreading walking through the door of my own home at the end of each day because of a disgusting old man.

Clay made an appointment with Dr. Rabin Stewart for the following Tuesday morning. As promised, he went with me but I was surprised to see when we arrived that he had not made the appointment for the *two* of us. We weren't going to be tackling this problem as a couple. Obviously, Clay was throwing this in my lap. His father, plus this horrible emotional abuse, equaled *my problem*. It was a stupid equation. The perverted old man was my burden and Clay was only going to make sure I had someone to talk to, since he was helpless to do anything but stand by as though he were an onlooker.

Weeks of therapy turned into months of therapy, but one thing remained the same, the victim had not been removed from the abusive situation, as the doctor suggested. The doctor challenged me to give my husband an ultimatum: his obviously troubled dad or his wife could live in that house—not both of us. Not at the same time. The doctor also suggested that Clay immediately seek medical help for Bernard before the situation escalated. I passed along the doctors suggestions to Clay and they fell on deaf ears. The doctor wanted to talk directly to Clay about it, but he refused. Week after week, I would leave therapy feeling that someone was on my side and that this situation was going to be taken care of once and for all—only to be let down as time passed and nothing was done. I eventually gave up hope that my husband was going to step up to the plate when it came to Bernard.

Clay's idea of solving the problem was not to cut out the tumor—his dad—but to stuff pills down my throat to stop the pain caused by the tumor. Looking back, I see that it was easier for Clay to shut me up than it was to begin World War III with his family, although, as we all know, *real* men, *brave* men, don't think twice about going in to battle. It's just what they do.

For six months during therapy, I was essentially being gutted with a knife and the good doctor was sewing me back together, only to have Bernard cut me open again the minute I got home. It was stupid and a waste of time, money and energy. I began to resent the way Clay refused to see his father for what he really was. I was furious that Clay didn't protect me from this monster.

Just Desserts

Six months after the fondling incident, Bernard suffered an abdominal aneurism and was in the hospital, near death, for two months. Clay didn't want his father to be alone, so from six in the morning until time to go to work in the afternoons, I sat at the hospital, reading novels and watching the life drain out of this man who hated me so much. In the very near future he would be dead and I would never know why he despised me. He would carry that secret into hell with him. So be it. For about one minute, I felt guilty that I was rejoicing the end of this cruel, insensitive monster's torturous reign.

While I dreaded the pain Clay would suffer at the loss, his father's impending doom left me feeling absolutely nothing. I always knew that I would finally be happy when I never had to look at his sorry face again, never had to hear him wish me dead. I watched over this sick old man who had hurt me so much only because I loved my husband and I would have done anything to make this difficult time easier for Clay.

At the same time, try as I might, I couldn't forgive his rotting soul for the damage he had done. Perhaps in time and with prayer and counseling I could release it, but right now this dark shroud threatened to be a constant presence until the unholy Bernard was dead and buried.

Clay took over for me at the hospital after lunch every day and sat with his father until 11PM when his brother would relieve him for the overnight shift. Rena, Clay's sister, was nowhere to be found during this entire ordeal. She was on an island cruise with some college friends when her father was sent to the hospital. Upon her return a week later, she didn't bother to visit nor did she offer to help me or her brothers with our vigil for the entire hospital stay.

Bernard asked to see Rena's husband, Therlow, in private and the two of them spent some time alone one afternoon as I waited in the hall. When Therlow came out of the room he looked at me as though he hated me. I wouldn't know until much later what had just transpired between the old man and his idiot son-in-law. With his dying breath, Bernard was laying the groundwork to bring his evil scheme full circle.

Doctors told the family that whether Bernard was sent to a nursing home or back to the house with a full-time medical care, he would need to be monitored around the clock for hemorrhaging. There wasn't a chance that he would ever have a normal life. He would be bed-bound and hooked to monitors and tubes for the remainder of his time here on earth.

The Will to Fight

Bernard Hutchison hung on to life for exactly six weeks after being brought home from the hospital. He hemorrhaged, just as the doctor predicted, and never regained consciousness. His funeral was attended by almost every farmer in the district along with a couple of legislators, a US senator, the mayor and other town hall dignitaries. Bernard had played an important role politically, especially during fund-raising events back in the day, and the beneficiaries of his generosity had come to pay their respects. It's a funny thing that money can buy respect—even for a disgusting, evil guy like old Bernie.

Man, if they only knew. No doubt, anything civil and decent that these politicians saw in Bernard was due to the graceful and highly intelligent woman by his side for so many gala political events—Ramona. It's very likely it was her money, not that of the parsimonious Bernard, that went into each candidate's coffers.

Atop the highest hill on Hutchison Farm, Bernard's body was put in a drawer beside Mrs. Hutchison's and above the vault of their little granddaughter's in the family mausoleum. Clay told me that Ramona had hired a contractor from Nashville to build the marble structure— very rare on a family plot—because she didn't like the idea of anyone in her family being put underground. As he told me about this, I pictured poor Ramona; her entire married life consumed with the idea of death and the wonderful escape she imagined it would be from her dreary existence.

In front of the giant marble building, surrounded by a large, black wrought-iron fence, were the graves of Clay's grandmother and grandfather Hutchison, one of their babies which was stillborn, Clay's Aunt Ruth who died in childbirth, along with her husband and one of her sons who had died of measles.

The family servants, an African-American man and his wife, who had worked faithfully on the farm for Clay's grandparents, were buried here with giant granite tombstones touting their beloved place in the hearts of this family.

After the brief graveside service, everyone walked back to the house where Clay's sister-in-law Elsa had catered a lavish reception for the funeral guests. Candles glowed in the silver candelabra and Ramona's Waterford crystal was brought into service. I could picture the genteel lady smiling down upon this crowd as they ate beef tenderloin from her heirloom English bone china and enjoyed the bounty of her elegant taste and exquisite style. In so many ways, I felt we were honoring Ramona more than we were mourning Bernard. That was appropriate.

In Middle Tennessee, it's customary for folks in the community to take a "covered dish" to the funeral home for the family. This was my first experience with a catered after-death event like this. I realize it was a *wake* as the northerners like to call it, but it looked more like a cocktail party. For me, it was a celebration of my new life—akin to my wedding reception. It was all I could do to hide my joy now that my abuser was gone. Psychologists tell the abused to "remove the victim." From this day forward, this victim could stay put.

Bernard was dead and now I could come to life and live in peace with Clay. Solitude was worth more to me than gold at this moment and I felt like wallowing in it for a while. I felt sorry for my husband who had lost his father, but purely glorious was that unmistakable feeling of freedom. I would never have to walk around that house in fear of being verbally attacked or physically assaulted ever again.

The family attorney gathered everyone around the dining table for the reading of Bernard's will, once the last reception guest had left. All members of the Hutchison family were there and accounted for. Even Rena, who had been noticeably absent during her father's illness, was front row center for the reading of her father's last will and testament.

Before the reading, however, the attorney wanted to meet with only Rena, Clay and Thomas behind the closed doors of the study. None of us knew what that was about, but Clay had tears in his eyes when Therlow, Elsa and I entered the room.

Each child received a lump sum of cash which was set up in an interest bearing account for his or her use and Clay got his father's part of the farm—which consisted of the original acreage, the tiny pre-civil war cottage, and the deed to the ranch house that Bernard and Ramona had built and maintained with Clay's help through the years. No one seemed upset and I assumed that Bernard had gone over his intentions with the family many years beforehand to ensure no one was surprised about their share of the lot. Rena and Therlow got a life-estate on the cottage, which meant they could stay there for the rest of their lives. Elsa and Thomas had a lifetime lease on the lot their house was built upon.

Poor Clay had worked for so many years and practically put his own life on hold to take this from a small family operation of seventy acres, to the giant, agri-business concern on 650+ acres that it was today. There wasn't much any of the other kids could say, except, "Thank you, Clay for allowing us to stay on your property," but, it had been the Hutchison compound for years and I suppose no one expected to be asked to leave.

I certainly didn't expect such a thing.

The New Normal

Shortly after Bernard's death, Clay began to feel a bit overwhelmed with the business of keeping the books, paying the hired hands, ordering tractor parts, and overseeing all the small details that his father had taken care of for him through the years. He asked me if I would be willing to quit my job and take over as "secretary, cook, homemaker, helpmate and love of his life," to quote him exactly. Who could resist such an offer from a gorgeous, hunky farmer who looked so sexy in a pair of jeans and wore a cowboy hat with the class of George Strait?

I turned in my notice at the factory after forty-two-plus years of punching somebody's time clock every day since I was a kid. I wasn't even tempted to look back.

This was the life I had dreamed of with Clay. I could now make a comfortable and happy home with my beautiful and loving man.

There were a few snags along the way—reminding me that Bernard's ghost was still hanging around somewhere. The most troubling was Clay's refusal to allow me to move our bed into the sprawling master bedroom suite where his father had slept. I hadn't laid eyes on this room until the day Bernard came home from the hospital. It was lovely. French doors opened to reveal a beautiful garden with a small fountain. "His and her" bathrooms were linked by a giant walk-in closet. There was a gas fireplace and a comfortable chaise lounge in a tiny reading nook near the bay window. Clay insisted that we turn the master suite into an office, instead. It made no sense, but I agreed, since he was so adamant about it. So, rather than taking over the room he deserved as the master of all he surveyed, we continued to sleep in his cramped little-boy room. He did allow me, after much cajoling, to get rid of his old twin beds that we had pushed together and replace them with a queen-sized canopy bed. At least I could lie there without the feeling I was falling into an abyss when I rolled over in my sleep.

For eight years after Bernard's death, Clay and I lived, loved, laughed and prospered on the farm. I organized my days perfectly. My farm chores, calls, and other responsibilities for the family business were finished by 11AM. Clay stopped work at midday for a nap and a healthy lunch which I had prepared after combing through Ramona's old cookbooks and family recipe cards.

My afternoons were filled with planning and getting dinner underway, along with the usual chores of laundry, ironing, making curtains, painting walls, cleaning rugs and scrubbing floors until they sparkled in this house which had ceased to recognize the passage of time. It seemed to me that Clay and his siblings looked upon this home as a shrine to their dead parents. Any drastic changes would have to be made at my own peril—but, oh, how I longed to burn that wagon wheel coffee table with the smoked glass top! I chose instead, to pick my battles when it came to decorating and rearranging the furniture.

Fridays were grocery days and I always went back to Tennessee for that. It gave me a chance to go to the beauty parlor, visit with my sister, and trade at the same market I had shopped in for decades.

On Wednesday evenings, Rena cooked dinner for all of us following church services and while she was her usual snobbish self, the food was delicious. After living with Bernard for the first few years of my marriage, I could put up with Lucifer himself for an hour.

This was my new normal.

Chips Off The Old Block

Time and a few strong cleaning products had wiped out the last physical traces and tobacco smells of the monster—the man who had made my life such a living hell in the first years of my marriage. Bernard was long gone, but in my most private moments, his horrible comments and actions would haunt me. I can't explain it. The nightmarish thoughts usually came back to me when Clay was away at the Arkansas stock sale and I was home alone and reading at night.

I always felt as though I was being watched and it sent chills up my spine. The cottage was next door and our living room side window looked right through to Rena's kitchen. There had never been curtains on this large bay window overlooking the rose garden between the houses, but it wasn't long before I decided there would have to be something on the windows if I was to have peace of mind. I installed some stylish matchstick Roman shades, which rather oddly, brought some rude and unsolicited remarks from Rena about my interior decorating ability. Her mean-spirited reaction made me wonder if Bernard had been telling me the truth about the rest of the family not wanting me here.

Turning Up The Heat

As the years passed, dinner on Wednesday nights at Rena's began to get more difficult to stomach and I'm not talking about the food. Rena, her obnoxious husband Therlow—who still wasn't speaking to me—along with Clay's brother, Thomas and his seemingly aloof wife, Elsa, sought out every opportunity to use their butter-knife sharp wit to criticize everything from my socks to my haircut and it seemed as though Clay never offered iodine for my wounds. Conversation at the dinner table never included me and if I did have the audacity to offer an opinion or comment about the topic of discussion, I got the look of daggers from Therlow and Rena. When I offered to help with dishes, I was shunned and practically driven from the kitchen as everyone whispered like cliquish children on the playground. I mentioned my disappointment about their behavior many times to Clay the next morning but he never had a single comment. He just shook his head and continued to read his paper as if I weren't in the room.

    I had given up on taking any kind of dish to this Wednesday night dinner long ago. One day I called Rena and asked what I could bring that evening as a contribution. She thought for a moment and told me it would be helpful if I would bring mashed potatoes. That night, as agreed, I showed up with steaming hot, buttered, mashed, golden potatoes which looked scrumptious.

Rena met us at the door with a turned up nose. She ignored me and asked Clay right in front of me what *his wife* could possibly be thinking when she showed up with mashed potatoes at a chili supper.

When I reminded Rena that she had requested the potatoes that morning, she brushed me off by saying that as the hostess, she reserved the right to change her mind about the menu without warning. I felt like dumping the entire bowl on her silly little head.

As time went on, the school girl games escalated until I was over it. My feelings were so hurt by Rena's remarks and her cruelty that I had lost my appetite anyway. Finally, it all came to a head when Rena stayed out on one of her "shopping trips" until after 6:30 on a wintery Wednesday evening. When the jealous and suspecting Thurlow came in from putting out hay and the house was dark and cold with nothing bubbling on the stove, the jig was up. She finally arrived home with an attitude and an announcement that Wednesday dinners at the Hutchison Compound were now someone else's responsibility—she was done. Elsa taught school and had papers to grade on Wednesday and then had early church. She certainly wasn't going to host a dinner. That left me.

I was thrilled to have the opportunity to play hostess and spent the next week looking through recipe books for just the right meal which would impress the in-laws. I invited everyone to our house for the following week and, much to my surprise, all agreed to join us.

We get the hint......

By Wednesday afternoon, pots were simmering on the stove, yeast rolls were rising, and there was a beautiful roast with carrots and potatoes in the oven. By 5:00, Clay had stopped his work, showered, and dressed for dinner. By 6:00, we were both looking out the window to see if our company was on the way. By 6:30, the appointed time for dinner, we phoned both couples and got no answer. Clay went over and no one came to the door when he knocked, even though he heard the television sets at both houses going at full volume. We phoned again to no avail.

By 7:00, Clay and I were enjoying a lovely meal and trying to figure out why we had been stood up by his rude family. Then, my sweet hubby shared with me something about his siblings that had been troubling him for quite some time.

Apparently, it was Rena and Thomas who suggested that Clay get a prenuptial agreement before our wedding. Clay thought they would drop it when he told them about his decision to marry me anyway, but they had not. Not only had they never stopped discussing the pre-nupt, but every day he was in their presence, they were hounding him about whether *he* had a last will and testament.

They told him that if something happened to him, the farm would go to me and they weren't going to sit still and allow that to happen. They asked him almost daily what he was going to do about the situation.

"What *are* you going to do about it, sweetheart?" I asked. "They aren't going to shut up about it until you have a will which protects them."

"It is my will that you would get the farm and that Rena and Thomas have a life-estate in their homes, just as they do now according to the original agreement set out in Dad's will," Clay explained. "You've been my wife for sixteen years and you deserve a place to live in case something happens to me. That's simply the way it's supposed to be. A man's wife inherits his estate."

"Clay, I appreciate that, but I can certainly understand their concerns as well," I tried to be the voice of reason. "There must be a way to compromise and make everyone comfortable with my being in your life," I continued, getting braver by the word. "You know, your dad told me every day that no one wanted me around and that I was in the way. He even said that everyone but you wished I would drop dead. Do you think their fears about the will could be the reason?"

I wanted to hear an explanation in Clay's own words. I was positive his siblings had not minced a syllable when they talked about their contempt of me. He wouldn't be able to play dumb with me this time. I wanted answers. Clay seemed ready to talk, but his words told me nothing.

"I don't know what it is, honey. I just know that every time I see either one of them they bring up the whole "will" thing. When Therlow is around, he chimes in with his ridiculous comments and he doesn't have a dog in this hunt. He keeps telling me that he knows something that I don't know and he acts like such a smug little jerk about it that I could throttle him. I don't know what the answer is, nor do I know what kind of settlement would possibly satisfy them." Clay seemed exhausted from discussing it.

Somehow, I could sense he wasn't telling me everything he knew. I had a feeling the family had said other unkind things about me that he didn't want to share. Secretly, I hoped that he had threatened to knock their blocks off for talking about his wife in an unflattering way. This was the man who had stood up to his own father for mistreating me. Surely he would thrash his brother–in-law if he got out of line.

"Let's find something good on TV tonight, okay, hon?" Clay looked totally beat as he abruptly changed the subject.

"You go ahead and put your feet up—I'll clear off the table and be right in to find a good movie for us." I smiled and forged ahead with my work, trying to forget the fact that I lived in the center of a busy hive and I was NOT about to be considered the queen bee by any of the Hutchisons, except for Clay.

From One Outsider to Another

After spending one crisp fall afternoon raking and bagging leaves, I was chilled to the bone and craving a nice pork loin with turnips and snap peas for our dinner. I had none of the ingredients, so I made a quick run to the market a few miles down the road. As I weighed a pound of peas and was looking at the Granny Smith apples for a big pie, I felt a hand on my back.

"Rose, are you looking for something warm to eat on this chilly day?" Elsa was standing next in line for the scales. She looked absolutely elegant in her leggings and a chunky wool tunic she had knitted herself. For the first time since I knew her, she had a pleasant look on her face. Almost as if she were happy to see me.

"Yes, I'm thinking pork loin with chutney and some turnips!" I chirped.

"Yum! I'll come to dinner at your house, then!" Elsa joked, almost forgetting that she and her husband had stood us up for dinner not so long ago.

"Eh…Rose…I hope you don't think I'm butting in to something that is none of my business, and I certainly won't be offended if you tell me to go away, but it's been almost sixteen years. When are you going to start speaking up in your marriage?"

I was floored. What on earth could Elsa mean by this?

"Speaking up? In my marriage?" I looked surprised, I'm sure.

"I happen to know that there's something going on that you do need to speak up about right away before it gets out of hand. Rena is pressuring Clay relentlessly about getting a last will and testament drawn up which would exclude you from getting any of his estate and would actually throw you off the farm in the event of his death. Are you aware of this? And, apparently, there is something in it for Therlow if you're completely out of the picture *before* Clay's death, Rose. Some kind of deal he cut with Bernard on his death bed," Elsa revealed matter-of-factly, as she put a pound of grapes on the scales.

"I was aware that Rena was pressuring Clay to get a will, but I had no idea she was asking him to leave me!" I said.

I was now hearing the small details that Clay was afraid to share. "The whole thing with Therlow and Bernard really bothers me. What could that be about, Elsa?"

Elsa placed the grapes in her cart and took my arm. "Rose, you need to knock on the door of that cottage and tell his sister and her redneck husband to butt out of your marriage and your financial business!" Elsa was very convincing and almost had me believing I could drum up the courage to do this with or without Clay's help.

"Let me know if I can help in any way, Rose. I just know that I had to stand up for myself in this family or Rena and the old man would have run me off the property years ago. The stakes are higher now that Clay owns the entire farm and they feel vulnerable. But, a life estate takes care of everything for everybody. We have our money. We have no children. As long as any of us are alive, you can't throw us out of our homes. You wouldn't do that anyway. They don't know the law and I guess they're frightened, that's all. Just don't let them wreck your marriage!"

I thanked Elsa for her kindness and, surprisingly, she gave me a hug and whispered she would be praying for all of this madness to pass.

Well, that's one I have on my side. Three to go. And to think, this is all because of something I hope I never live to see, my husband's last will and testament being read in front of a group of vultures. If something were to happen to my beloved Clay, I wouldn't want to go on anyway. I couldn't imagine life without Clay. It certainly wouldn't be worth living if I knew I would never see him again.

Hatching a Plan

I shuddered at the thought of something happening to the love of my life. How could his siblings be so obsessed with something so morbid? I climbed out of my funk when I realized I still had a romantic dinner for two to plan for this evening. I would set the table in front of the fireplace and put on some soft music. Clay will be coming in from feeding the livestock on this chilly night and he'll catch a whiff of this fabulous meal on the stove. He needs comfort food and he needs to feel my arms around him. This will set the stage for me to share Elsa's ideas about this problem which has been consuming his sister and brother since the day we married. I'll tell him that Elsa is on our side and he'll be pleased that we have someone with some intelligence in our corner. This is going to be a great night!

The Best Laid Plans....

After our sumptuous dinner, Clay was ready to relax in front of the fireplace with a glass of wine but I was ready to invite the rest of the clan over for coffee and a little remedial instruction on "Butting Out 101." He reluctantly agreed with the caveat that it would do absolutely no good to tell Rena to mind her own business at this juncture. She had been meddling all of her life and she wasn't going to change.

I wasn't hearing any of Clay's excuses. I was buoyed by Elsa's pep talk in the grocery store and felt I had a comrade in arms should I get up the courage to call them all over here for a family meeting. Before my determination waned, I picked up the phone and dialed Rena and Therlow to ask them over for coffee.

"We need to talk." I confidently announced the instant Rena picked up the phone.

"I don't see any reason why we should talk, Rose," Rena shot back rudely.

"We'll all feel better after we clear the air, Rena. Clay and I really want you to come over," I said. Rena hung up the phone without another word.

Next, I called my ally, Elsa, but got Thomas on the phone instead.

"Elsa's at a PTA meeting and I'm tired. Some of us work all day, Rose!" Thomas never missed an opportunity to chastise me for quitting my job at the factory.

"Please, Thomas. Clay wants everyone to come because there's something we need to discuss."

Thomas also hung up the phone without saying a word.

Within ten minutes, Rena, Therlow and Thomas were in our kitchen and refused my offer for coffee and comfortable chairs in the living room. They stood, propped up along the kitchen counters, as if they had read in some book that a meeting would be shorter this way. Sensing that his family was being uncooperative, Clay came in and sat at the kitchen table with his coffee. I continued to stand since I was going to moderate this meeting. I had read the same office management book.

"Okay, Rose, why did you call hard working people out on this cold-ass night?" Thomas rolled his eyes and leaned back against the fridge.

Feeling every bit as courageous as I felt after talking to Elsa in the grocery store, I got right to the point. "Rena, how long have you been talking to Clay about getting a will? Don't you think that's a private matter between a husband and his wife? After all, that's nothing a husband would talk to his sister about, anyway."

Rena laughed and looked at Therlow.

Therlow shook his head and his face began to redden. His stubby little legs took less than two steps to reach me and he shoved his fist right under my nose. I was taller than he, so I had to look down at him. It would have been comical had it not been so tragic and so completely redneck.

"I can tell you exactly how long it's been," he whispered. "It's been sixteen long years that we've been tryin' to get rid of you, bitch!"

I took a step back and shot a look at Clay who was gazing upon this vulgar scene with the same emotion he would muster had he been watching it on the Jerry Springer Show.

Some munchkin has his fat fist in the wife's face and the husband watches with no emotion whatsoever. This is just great.

"After whut you've done to this family, you don't deserve one damn thang that we' all got down here!" With that, Therlow completed his rant, walked out and slammed the kitchen door behind him. Rena followed him without a word. How proud she must be of that little man!

"This ain't over, Rose. You've got to understand. Therlow and Rena are in this to win," Thomas chimed in as he headed for the door.

"Elsa is on my side!" I shot back.

"Elsa is a much of an outsider as you are," Thomas said, and he walked out the door leaving me alone to stare at this stranger sitting at the kitchen table. Clay is my *husband* and he's supposed to defend me. He should have helped me in this discussion. He did nothing when his brother-in-law threatened me with his fist! What a wuss!

Clay must have felt my icy stare. He walked to the sink and looked out the window.

"Clay, are you mad at me for confronting Rena with this?" I asked.

"I should have knocked the hell out of Therlow." Clay said, as he watched his brother make his way home. Thomas would have belted Therlow if he had held his fist to Elsa's face. Clay knew that as well as I did.

"No, I don't want you fighting in our home, okay?" I tried to comfort him, but the tears from my disappointment began to flow. I ran to the bedroom and buried my head in the pillow, sobbing in anger and frustration. As I lay there in the dark, my mind went back in time.

My mind went back to the many years of dating Clay—all our good times and our laughter and quiet, romantic dinners. I married this man because I love him with all my heart. He's always told me that I am the love of his life. Where does his family fit in to this picture?

Why is he so afraid to stand up to them? How could any real man sit still and allow his brother-in-law to insult and threaten his wife? There was a very good chance that I didn't know this man at all.

I could hear the television in the living room down the hall. Clay was watching one of his detective shows and probably wasn't giving the events of this evening one more thought. I could think of little else. I was disappointed. I was stunned. Then, all that had been said began to ring in my ears.

Thomas said that if Elsa took up for me, it was only because she was an outsider too. Therlow said 'after what you've done to this family.' I've done nothing but love Clay. What have I done to the family by simply loving my husband? So much greed—so much hatred from these awful people that lived within a stone's throw of me! If Clay didn't defend me in our own home, he must not be standing up for me each day when his family stabs me in the back.

I cried until I couldn't cry any more, got up and ran a hot bath, took one of my sleeping pills, and was out for the night. I couldn't bear to give this mess one more minute of my time. I would call Elsa the next day and tell her what happened. She could advise me. Maybe I should have sought Elsa's help from the beginning, many years ago. It certainly would have saved me a great deal of pain.

As if nothing happened....

The next morning, Clay was his usual loving, attentive self. He got up early to make breakfast and met me at the kitchen table with a kiss and the newspaper. I could tell he was nervous because he was into this manic chattering about the weather and the big arctic front that was coming toward the state. It was though he was marking time to fill every bit of air space—anything to keep me from bringing up the uncomfortable events of the night before. I didn't want to talk about it either. What was there left to say? I had surmised that I was the odd man out in this big Hutchison family compound and I was going to have to get used to that. I would never be accepted as part of the family. I would always be thought of as the interloper—the outsider.

All the love Clay could pour from his heart could do nothing to change these circumstances for me. But our marriage vows were for better or worse, for richer, for poorer. I didn't want Rena's stupid house, her money, her stocks or her sad life. I didn't want anything that belonged to anyone else. I just wanted to be left alone with Clay, in our house, with our lives together and our love for each other. Why was that too much to ask? Why is it that when a couple says "I do," they're making that lifetime vow to an entire, screwed-up, dysfunctional, family?

I promised myself that I would never bring up the subject again. Since I didn't want to discuss a will or anything closely related to Clay's death anyway, it wasn't a difficult promise to keep. I immersed myself in cooking, cleaning, doing my crafts, reading and sewing. In the spring, I spent hours in the flower garden tending the beautiful roses, pulling weeds and combing the garden books for heirloom seeds and cuttings to order.

For the next few months, I could count on one hand the number of times I laid eyes on Rena, Therlow or Thomas. Once in a while, Elsa would sneak over and have tea in the afternoons, but she would have to keep a keen eye out the window for her husband's return. Heaven forbid if she's caught talking to the enemy! Elsa agreed that I was in a difficult spot and to keep Clay happy, I should keep quiet and keep a watchful eye on Therlow. She despised him and didn't put anything past him or Rena and that thought made me uneasy.

Clay and I went to church almost every Sunday and spent the afternoons browsing in antique shops or just lounging around watching the big game or doing crossword puzzles. I pretended that the people who lived next door to us, Rena and Therlow, were strangers— strangers whose dog had attacked my cat and weren't allowed to speak to me for legal reasons. That way of thinking seemed to work for me. Elsa was on my side and I think she had softened Thomas' opinion of me as time went by. As for Clay, he had to get along with Therlow and Thomas since they each owned one-third of the cattle.

Reaching Out From the Grave

One fall afternoon, Clay was attending the stock sale in the next county and I was spending my day in the root cellar organizing the canned goods, taking inventory and getting the storage area prepared for several batches of pickles and peaches I had canned. The root cellar was huge and was dug by men who worked the farm long before the Hutchisons lived there. It was lined in dressed rock which had been honed by slaves when the property was a big plantation in the 1800's. Above it, the large wooden structure that housed the tractors and the many farm implements it took to cultivate 650 acres. Fencing was stored here and there was a workshop where blades were sharpened and broken plows repaired. Thomas and Therlow considered this building their "office."

I had been quietly working in the cellar all morning and it soon became quite obvious that no one knew I was down there. These two rode in on a large John Deere tractor and brought in a sickle mower which apparently had broken in half as they cut hay in a small pasture.

Their banter was mostly about the stubborn nuts and bolts on the piece of machinery, but then all must have worked out because the cursing subsided and gave way to a frank discussion on the subject they loved to hate: what to do about Rose.

I held my breath to listen. Perhaps I would finally learn about this big family secret that had been held over my head since the old man's death. I had waited so patiently and had prayed for just one piece of this puzzle which had eluded me for so many years. Why did they hate me? Why had Therlow not spoken to me except to threaten me since the day he sat vigil at old man Hutchison's death bed?

"Did Rena talk to Clay last night?" Thomas spoke first.

"Yep. I think she finally got it through his thick skull that it's way past time," Therlow laughed.

"What's he gonna do?"

"He said he'd handle it."

"Did she tell him about what Daddy told you? About Rose hitting him in the abdomen with her fist all the time and causing the aneurism?"

"Yeah, and how she beat up on him all those years when Clay left the house," Therlow grunted.

I almost gasped out loud and bit into my hand to keep them from hearing me under the thin board floor. Oh my God! That son-of-a-bitch Bernard! He's reaching out from the grave to hurt me with his lies and cruelty.

"You know Clay! He didn't say a thang," continued Therlow. "Then, I reminded him there was another reason to get rid a' her that was even more important than that crap."

"The money?" asked Thomas.

"Yep. You guys have been a lot more patient that I woulda been, but Clay's not my brudder. I just know if somebuddy had left me $250 thou just to get rid of my old lady, no offense about yore sister an' all, but I'd 'a dumped Rena like a bad habit."

"Yeah, we know that about you, Therlow. Part of your charm. Just so you know, that money's got the kid's names on it—not yours, and not Elsa's. And it all depends on what Clay does. I say he doesn't have the balls to do it and I'd be willing to wager you my part of the tobacco crop that it won't be done this time next year. What do ya wanna bet? But, in the scheme of things, what does it matter if we get to stay here the rest of our lives anyway?" Thomas asked.

"I'm freakin' broke," said Therlow. "That's why I wish the asshole would hurry up and lose that bitch. We can't wait for her to croak on her own. That bitch'll outlive all of us."

"Well, I don't think Clay has the balls. Never has. Biggest wuss that's ever had the name Hutchison. They used to steal his money and stuff him in the locker after baseball practice and he was too scared to even tell Daddy about it," recalled Thomas. "He wouldn't tell her to take a hike if he caught both of us in bed with her!"

"I wouldn't screw her with that little thang you got!" Therlow chuckled. "But just 'cause Clay is a damn coward don't mean we have to suffer does it? Whew! That feisty old diddie a yores! How come if she hit him he didn't whoop her ass? That bitch better not cross me, I'll knock her into next week with this hammer! I might anyway. Hasten thangs up a lil," Therlow bragged.

I was sitting on the floor holding my stomach and trying to keep from throwing up. I was terrified. Bernard had lived long enough to spew his venomous lies and he was haunting me still. What Therlow was hinting about was unthinkable. He wants me to die. And if it's not of natural causes so be it. He's just greedy enough to hasten my end along, and we were so far out in the country, who would know? Clay wasn't expected home for hours and if Therlow discovered me here in the cellar—if he knew I had overheard their conversation—he might be tempted to take his talk about getting rid of me to the next level. I sat as still as I could and prayed they would leave soon.

It was a hot fall day and I was in a root cellar shivering from cold, fright, and an emotion I couldn't name. It was another miserable hour before the two men left the tractor shed and drove back out into the field to finish their mowing. I ran back to the house and deadbolted the door to compose myself and decide what to do. Clay was unreachable—this was in the era before everyone had a cell phone. I *had* to talk to Clay. Only he could help me understand this. Only he could make this right.

In the next instant, I was furious with my husband. How could he have a conversation like that with Therlow and not come directly to me to get my side of the story? How long ago was this?

Did Clay actually believe I had abused his disgusting father? The thought made me feel, once again, as if I needed to vomit. The mere thought that the old man hinted to Therlow that I had hit him and caused his aneurism was almost too much to comprehend for a woman who had only been around genteel, kind, and honest people all of her life.

It was all becoming very clear to me now. That's why Therlow looked so angry when he left Bernard's hospital bedside. Therlow believed I had physically abused an elderly man, when in reality, it was the other way around and Clay could have set him straight.

And the trust fund! That's what the meeting prior to the reading of the will was all about. The dirty old man had apparently set up a fund of $250 thousand dollars which none of the kids could touch until Clay got me out of his life. And what was in it for Therlow? Had Bernard offered him even more money to talk Clay into leaving me?

So, that's what made "getting rid of Rose" the family affair that it had become all these years. It was all beginning to make sense. I wondered if Elsa knew about any of this. Her husband knew, obviously, but I hadn't noticed any change in her actions toward me. If anything, Elsa had become more of a friend since the old man's death. What did she have to gain by befriending me if she had heard—and believed—the old man's lies from the grave?

The Gas Lighting Begins

By the time Clay got home from the stock sale that afternoon, my emotions had been alternating between terror and extreme anger for close to four hours. My heart was racing and I was weak from pacing back and forth. I had no appetite and didn't think I would ever want to eat again. Starting dinner for Clay was the last thing on my mind. I'm sure he thought it was odd when he walked in to the house and I wasn't at the stove stirring a pot.

"Honey, I'm home! Rosie! Hey sweetheart! Where are you?" Clay was turning on lights as he passed through the house looking for me.

"I'm in here, Clay," I answered calmly.

Clay didn't know what to make of me sitting in the living room in the dark.

"Hey, sweetie! I brought you some sunflowers from the farmer's market," Clay said, as he entered the room. His expression changed when he clicked on the lamp beside my chair and saw my tear-stained face and my clenched jaw.

"Oh, honey! What's wrong? Are you okay?"

I stared into Clay's eyes for what must have seemed like an eternity to him—I didn't know where to begin. The frustration caused the tears to flow. As I sobbed, Clay reached out to hold me and without thinking, I pushed him away.

"Why didn't you TELL me?" I demanded to know. "Why didn't you TELL me about your Daddy's horrible lies? Why didn't you TELL me that your family wanted me dead all along?"

"What in the world are you talking about, Rose?" Clay sat on the ottoman in front of me.

"I heard Therlow and Thomas talking today, Clay. I heard it all. I just want to know why you didn't share this with me. I'm your WIFE DAMMITT!" I stood up and screamed out my frustrations—glad at that particular moment I had installed the shades on the big bay window to keep Rena's prying eyes out of my marriage.

"Now, exactly what do you think you heard, Rose?" The way Clay couched his question fueled the fire within me. What did I *think* I heard? How dare him!

An old movie reel churned in my head. In this classic from 1944, Ingrid Bergman plays a woman whose husband tries to make her believe she's going insane. "Gaslight" is the name of the film and the term became iconic in our language whenever people were told they were "imagining" things that were in fact, quite real.

"I heard, Clay—I heard very clearly! On his damned death bed, Bernard told Therlow that I had physically abused him since I moved in and that I caused his aneurism!" I screamed.

"Clay, Do *you* believe the sick, twisted, lies of your evil father?"

Clay sat there, motionless, with that blank stare on his face that I had come to know so well.

"Do you hear me? Did you know about this lie?" I demanded an answer.

He continued to stare straight ahead as if in a hypnotic trance. I grabbed his arm and squeezed it to get his attention. "Well, then, can you answer this Clay? Why didn't you tell me after the will was read that your sadistic daddy left a quarter of a million in a trust on the condition that you *get rid of me*? What the hell is *that*?" My anger was escalating as the blank look on Clay's face did not change.

"I want answers Clay! If I have to sit here all night screaming at you, I'm going to get those answers," I warned. "I suffered through your father's sick abuse and disrespect for years because I didn't want to hurt you— didn't want to lose you. And now *this*? He's turning it around on me from the grave!" I screamed.

"Now, honey," Clay whispered in a very low voice that sounded like a remote-controlled robot.

"We sometimes think we hear certain things when we walk into the middle of someone else's conversation. Right now, you need to calm down, let's get something to eat and we'll figure this out. You're upset right now. Have you had your pills today? I hate to see you this upset—it isn't good for your heart, honey," Clay was patronizing me and I was livid. There were a lot of things going on around here that weren't good for my heart. He was quickly becoming one of them.

"I know what I heard Clay. I'm perfectly sane. I'm not taking pills and I didn't walk in on someone's conversation. I was in the root cellar, perfectly alert and I heard Therlow and Thomas talking as plainly as you and I are talking now. Don't you dare try to get out of helping me with this Clay!"

"Honey, we'll talk to the doctor in the morning together and see what's going on with you. I hate to see you like this."

I could not believe what was happening right in front of me.

Clay was in total denial. I was the dummy here, or so his family would like for me to think. I was the paranoid wife who *imagined* that the old man was emotionally abusing *her*. I was the paranoid sister-in-law who *imagined* that her in-laws didn't like her. I was the scared little country mouse who *imagined* I was being treated like an outcast in this family.

It's interesting that I had i*magined* all these things after decades of living a perfectly sane, single, and responsible adulthood. I had to get involved with Clay Hutchison and his family of rodeo clowns before I officially lost my marbles.

With Clay's dismissal of my feelings and his patronizing treatment eating at me, I ran down the hall and shut myself up in the bedroom. I had to get away from him. I didn't even want to see his face right now. I felt safe in the cocoon of the soft, comfortable bed. Here, I could gather my thoughts and determine my next move.

But what on earth would that be? With each passing year, my options had dwindled because I had pitched my tent for Clay and had given up everything in my life for him, as wives from my generation usually did.

While I still owned my little home in Lafayette, I had practically given it to my sister and her daughter since they had nowhere to go after her divorce. I gave up my job and my friends to make my life here in this strange town with even stranger people.

If Clay were to toss me away like yesterday's meat loaf, who is going to hire a fifty-eight year old woman with no skills? The automotive plant had moved out of Lafayette years ago and there were no factories left. Very few restaurants would think of hiring a woman my age to wait tables. I was in great shape and worked out every day, but being on my feet for an eight hour shift would be taxing.

Then, thankfully, I stopped myself from going down that road.

Oh, for Pete's sake! What was I doing? This way of thinking isn't like me at all. I'm always the one who looks on the positive side—but at the same time, I'm pragmatic, so maybe that part of my personality is kicking in to help me solve this problem. As I lay in the dark, confused, hurt and trying to find a trace of an option, another part of my personality kicked in: anger.

I finally decided that I'd had a bellyful of Clay's passive behavior when it came to his family. He wasn't being a man. He was that helpless a little boy again who had no control when it came to his older siblings who acted like mafia dons. Rena and Thomas, and to a bigger extent, Therlow, were bullies. They were losers because none of them had bothered to give up their social lives to earn money and plan for the future as Clay did. They were spoiled frat and sorority kids who came back to reap the benefits of their sweet little brother's hard work here on this farm.

I tossed and turned in the darkness for several hours until Clay tiptoed past the bed and slipped into the bathroom to brush his teeth and get into his pajamas. I wasn't about to say another word to him. The ball was in his court and it was up to him to get to the bottom of this mess and straighten out his sick, greedy, hot-mess of a family.

Once Clay came to bed and rolled over with his back to me, I sprang up to run a bubble bath. At least I could waste time until Clay was asleep and I wouldn't have to lie there and put up with more of his annoying silence. After a long soak, I took one of my allergy capsules and I was down for the count. Perhaps when I awoke, I would learn this was all a horrible nightmare.

As If Nothing Happened…..

The sun's rays streamed through the windows of the bedroom and directly into my eyes the next morning. I hadn't shut the blinds last night because I obviously had too much on my mind. Clay was already up and I could hear him running water and shuffling pots and pans in the kitchen. Suddenly, a pain in the pit of my stomach reminded me of the events of the day before. This had to be addressed today. It could not be put off one more hour. We needed to call a family meeting immediately to clear my name of Bernard's lies. I got dressed and made my way to the kitchen with the hope that Clay had everything under control and had scoped out a plan of action.

"Good morning, my love!" Clay pulled out the chair at the kitchen table with one hand, while pouring my coffee with the other. He bent down to kiss me and I turned my cheek to him.

"What are we going to do about this, Clay?" I said in my most businesslike tone.

"Do about what, my love?" He loaded my plate with a stack of blueberry pancakes. "Now, don't those look great?"

"You know good and well what I'm talking about." I asserted.

"Oh, you mean that load of garbage from Therlow and Thomas? Don't you know by now that they're just trouble-makers who are so jealous of what we have that they can't stand it?"

I was relieved to hear that Clay agreed these were all lies, but I wasn't so happy with his matter-of-fact tone. It seemed to me that he was ready to dismiss what had happened to me as a sibling rivalry out on the playground. It infuriated me to think he was going to let it go.

"Clay, what about the money your father is holding back from everyone—the money that can't be touched until you get me out of your life?"

"Oh, honey, that's not what they were talking about. You must have heard them wrong. They were apparently referring to the life estates or something. I know nothing of any money attached to my getting "rid" of you. Do you think I would sit still for that?" Clay took my hand and leaned across the table to kiss me. "There's not enough money in this world for me to give up the love of my life."

Something in me melted. We kissed and I looked into my darling's beautiful pale blue eyes.

"If you tell me it's so, then I'll believe you, Clay."

"Mrs. Hutchison, I want to take you away from here on a real adventure," Clay changed the subject so abruptly it startled me. "We've never had a real honeymoon and I thought we could go to an island somewhere and feel the sand in our toes." Clay laughed as he clasped my hand tightly.

"What brought that on so quickly?" I asked.

In sixteen years of marriage, Clay Hutchison has never wanted to leave the state of Kentucky. This was quite a departure.

"You've been through so much. I want to take you away from all this. Away from this compound, away from everyone else's drama. For once in our lives I just want us to feel as though we're the only two people on the face of the earth," Clay suddenly got very melancholy. He looked down at our hands, still intertwined.

"Well, if you agree to go along with me on this adventure, I'll make all the necessary arrangements today. Is your dance card full next week? We both smiled as we remembered he had asked me that same thing the first time he called so many years ago.

"For you, my love, I'll clear my calendar for the rest of the month, but I'll only go away with you on one condition," I said. "On the condition that you march over there right now and tell Thomas and Therlow you don't want to hear them spreading any more of Bernard's nasty lies about your wife."

"That's the first thing on my agenda this morning," Clay assured me. "I should have set them straight a long time ago, but I have a feeling they won't be bothering us anymore." With that, he kissed me and I was confident that this whole nasty episode was behind us.

If you're grading me here, give me a big, fat, "F" on *follow-up*.

The Perfect Honeymoon

Clay wanted to surprise me, so he refused to give me a hint about where we were going until we got to the airport and I overheard him tell the ticket agent we were flying to Miami. I would have been happy with that since I had never been there, but as I found out when we landed, that wasn't our destination. Once in Miami, we rented a convertible and drove south to a little Tiki bar and restaurant, far beyond Seven-Mile Bridge and just north of Key West. At that restaurant, we parked the car, grabbed our luggage, and boarded a ferry to a privately owned resort called "Little Palm Island."

This exclusive resort accommodates only twenty couples at a time in little private luxury villas with thatched roofs and hammocks on sparkling white sand. A world-renowned chef serves up gourmet meals especially for the island guests. As our ferry arrived, I noticed that a large private yacht was docked out front and several couples were sitting in beach chairs under giant yellow umbrellas. This was paradise—my dream getaway—everything I imagined a honeymoon should be. For the coming week, we were newlyweds who had been married for sixteen years.

Like a blushing new bride, I was seeing a different side of this handsome man with me. I was observing my husband out of his comfort zone of the farm for the first time, and I was learning so many things about him that I never even knew to ask. I had no idea Clay knew so much about the ocean and its inhabitants. I learned that he used to be a voracious reader of travel books and as a child, he entertained the thought of becoming an oceanographer after watching a documentary about Jacques Cousteau on PBS. Seeing this side of him, away from his family, against the backdrop of this island paradise, I was falling in love with him all over again.

We walked hand in hand along the beach, relaxed by the pool, drank Pina Coladas garnished with little paper umbrellas and ate fresh pineapples and mangoes. Clay patiently taught me to snorkel and we rented an underwater camera to take photos of the colorful fish and coral down below. We wisely paced ourselves since we weren't accustomed to the strong tropical sun, and by the end of the week, we were both as brown as biscuits and as limp as noodles—especially after sitting in the hot tub drinking Sangria until midnight.

Getting away was just what we needed. It occurred to me that this was another first for us: the first time we had been really alone for more than one night in our entire marriage.

Bernard was around, spreading his pox for so many years, and then, there were those four people permanently camped on the compound. Not exactly a recipe for romance. Unfortunately, we would never be completely free of them, but right now, on this island, they didn't exist.

As far as we were concerned, there was only one couple on earth with a strong bond no one could break. The abuse, the hatred, and the lies, Bernard and his devilish schemes—they were gone forever—washed out to sea with the tide never to be seen again.

Back to Reality

When we climbed aboard the ferry and said goodbye to our island getaway, we were so sad, but you wouldn't have known that by looking at us. Dressed in our cargo shorts, t-shirts and flip-flops, we looked like old surfer-dudes with dark, reddish-brown skin, peeling noses and permanent smiles etched on our faces. We waved goodbye to our ferry captain and promised to come back to this fabulous resort for our twentieth anniversary. This would be our place from now on. The photos from our belated honeymoon would go into our wedding album to be enjoyed when we were too old to snorkel, too senile to drive, and our bones to brittle to risk physical contact.

We arrived at the farm still decked out in our shorts and T-shirts a little after midnight and found everything to be in order, just as we left it. Feeling the cold against our almost sunburned skin was excruciating and neither of us had given any thought to what the weather would be like when we landed. We were in the frame of mind that our world was sunny, warm and 85 degrees no matter where we went.

Clay brought our luggage in from the car, but we were both too exhausted to unpack. I would do that tomorrow and put in a load of clothes before I went grocery shopping. There was nothing in the house to eat, and just like a new homemaker, I would have to stock up on everything in town tomorrow. I reached into my purse and pulled out the treasure—a huge stack of beautiful photographs of our vacation. I had them developed in the gift shop before we checked out and we had enjoyed them on the plane. It was going to be so much fun to look through these again and again, re-living this time in our lives as the years passed. I found my favorite photo of the two of us and stuck it on the fridge with a magnet. Clay will get a kick out of this!

Our Summer Is Over

Clay and I were subconsciously still on vacation and terribly jet-lagged. We remained in bed in a coma-like state until I woke up and looked at the clock around 9 AM. I gently kissed my handsome husband on the back of his neck to wake him and he rolled over. As we usually only had time for on Saturdays, we romantically extended the honeymoon for a while longer. Afterwards, we were starving. I mixed up some blueberry jam-macadamia nut pancakes from scratch and Clay went for his morning jog. We seemed to be getting back to our morning routine without skipping a beat.

We enjoyed our breakfast slowly and quietly. Coming down from this "honeymoon high" was going to be more difficult than either of us had imagined. Clay even looked a little depressed.

"How about if I grill up some teriyaki chicken for supper tonight with fresh pineapple and wild rice, just like we had on the island?" I hoped my suggestion would prolong our "vacation feeling" for one more night and put a smile on Clay's face.

"Whatever you want to do, honey, will be fine with me. You're tired. I can get some take–out from Joe's Bar-b-cue and bring it home for us if you're too exhausted to cook," Clay sweetly offered.

"No, honey, I insist. I'm ready to get back in the saddle and make dinner for my handsome husband in my beautiful kitchen. I feel like we got married last weekend!" I chirped.

Clay got up from the table and, as he always did, complimented me on a delicious breakfast. Then, he took me in his arms and held me tighter than he's ever held me before.

"I love you so damn much, Rose Hutchison! Don't you ever, ever forget that as long as you live, you promise? I'll see you tonight," Clay continued to hold me in the tight bear hug. It was as though he never intended to let go.

"I love you *more*, my darling! Don't you ever forget that, Clay Hutchison," I kissed him on the neck and turned his face to look into his beautiful eyes. Tears were starting to well-up and when I saw that, it made my tears flow as well. Could two people be any more in love?

With a quick peck on my cheek, he grabbed the truck keys, climbed in the pick-up, and headed down the driveway. I sprinted to the kitchen window like a school girl to watch my love leave to begin his day of farm work. This is what it's all about. In his wisdom, Clay knew we needed to escape and remind ourselves of why we fell in love in the first place.

After all the tears, pain and lies from people who made no difference one way or another, we had found our way back to true intimacy. Our vacation might be over—but our summer was just beginning. We were like two kids on the last day of school who were looking forward to a world of adventure ahead.

I had a feeling deep in my heart that we had turned a corner in our relationship. This honeymoon had brought us closer than we've ever been and, presenting a unified front, we would be able to knock down any wall that nutty family of his tried to build between us in the future. Clay had that power over me. Whenever he said "I love you Rose," it energized me and gave me the courage to conquer the world. Perhaps now, my love for him would help him find the strength to stand up to his siblings who had a history of making everyone else miserable.

I jumped in the shower and got comfortably dressed for my long list of errands and shopping. Our "island dinner" tonight was going to be so much fun. I sailed out the door on a cloud to begin my busy day.

I wasn't about to give negative thoughts one more minute of my time. I popped in a Jimmy Buffet cassette, turned it up full blast, and sang along as I drove to Lafayette and visited with my sister before my hair salon appointment and shopping. I couldn't wait to show her our vacation photos. She was so proud of the 5x7 seashell frame I brought her from the Little Palm Island gift shop. Included as a bonus, was a shot of Clay and his fifty-something beach bum bride, sitting in beach chairs, sipping on cocktails. I filled her in on all the fabulous details and told her of our plans to go back to "Our Island," as Clay and I would call it from now on.

Are You Rose Hutchison?

With my sun-bleached hair trimmed and styled and my grocery shopping completed, I glanced at the clock as I pulled in to the farm entrance and headed up the steep hill to the house. Good. It was only 4:30. I had plenty of time to unpack our things, put in several loads of laundry, freshen up the house and fire up the grill before Clay finished his work. I looked at the houses on each side of ours—good. No one was home at either place. This must be my lucky day.

As I got to the top of the hill, my heart almost stopped.

Parked in front of the house was a deputy from the sheriff's department. Oh my God! Has something happened to Clay? Did he have an accident on the tractor? I shot out of my car almost before it stopped rolling and ran to the cruiser as the deputy climbed out.

"Are you Rose Hutchison?" I could barely hear him as his radio crackled and rumbled in the background. He closed the car door and spoke some kind of code into the microphone mounted on his shoulder. He never took his eyes off me as he waited for my answer.

"Yes, I'm Rose," I choked on my words, feeling almost nauseous.

"Mrs. Hutchison, could we step inside the house to talk a moment, please?"

"What is this about?" I fumbled with the keys and opened the front door. As the cops like to say, the deputy "remained silent," while my heart was beating out of my chest in horrible anticipation. I motioned for him to sit on the living room sofa.

I didn't see the truck. Where was Clay!? It then occurred to me that it was odd that Clay's siblings and their spouses weren't home this time of day. My mind was reeling as I sat down.

"Mrs. Hutchison, I have some papers I need you to take a look at here for just a moment," he said. He opened a manila envelope and his beefy hands brought out a thick stack of stapled documents. I let out a sigh of relief.

Praise God! He wasn't here to give me the horrible news that Clay was in an accident or had been found lifeless under a tractor somewhere. Oh Thank God!

"Now, Mrs. Hutchison, you've probably been expecting this, but I'm going to explain it to you and walk you through it just to make it official," he politely smiled. "By the way, I'm Deputy Randall Bryant of the Adair County Sheriff's Department."

Almost immediately, it flashed through my mind that Rena and Thomas were behind this. These papers were something they wanted me to sign. This was their end game. It was some kind of Quit Claim Deed or some document asking me to swear in a court of law that I wouldn't take a nickel of Clay's money in the event of his death. Oh they had the nerve. Clay is going to outlive us all, you jerks!

"Okay, what do my crazy in-laws have in store for me now?" I chuckled and rolled my eyes.

"Mrs. Hutchison, it's my duty to inform you that you are being served. Mr. Clay Hutchison is seeking a divorce on the grounds of irreconcilable differences in the courts of Adair County, Kentucky," the words rolled off his tongue as though he had been practicing the lines his entire life—waiting for just this moment.

I went numb. I don't remember if I said anything. I do recall looking at the top of the paper as he handed it to me, my eyes riveted on "Clay Martin Hutchison vs. Rose Reid Hutchison."

My mouth was parched and I slowly rose from the sofa, not taking my eyes off the paper.

"I need some water, deputy, would you like something?" I almost choked because a lump was starting to form in my throat. I didn't want to cry in front of this stranger. But, oddly, I didn't feel as though I was going to cry. I couldn't feel anything. This was just a big mistake. A cruel joke that was so much like something his tacky family would do. Like Elsa warned me, don't put anything past any of them.

I walked into the kitchen to grab a bottle of water from the fridge and my eyes caught the vacation photo I had stuck on the door last night. I had put it there for Clay to see every day when he came home to lunch. We're so happy and so in love in this photo! This isn't happening. There has to be some mistake. This is indeed the work of

Rena and Thomas. They had these papers drawn up while Clay and I were on the island! This must be the case.

Suddenly, I felt very silly. I sat at the table to begin searching the documents for the name of the attorney who drew up these phony papers. I was going to call him and find out who had been in his office and when.

As I got up to find the phone book, Clay pulled into the driveway and the garage door slowly opened. Oh, Thank God. My dear husband will straighten all this out. He'll explain everything and the deputy can be on his way, serving some other poor soul whose marriage *really* is over. Deputy Bryant suddenly appeared in the doorway and pulled up a chair at the kitchen table.

Clay walked in, stopped abruptly, and gave me a look I'll never forget as long as I live. He didn't have to say a word. In his eyes, I saw the truth. The papers were apparently, very real. We stared at each other in uncomfortable silence.

"Clay, what is this?" I was finally able to choke out. "What have you done, sweetheart?" Now, my tears were flowing freely .

"I didn't know what else to do," he said as he looked down at the floor, unwilling to make eye contact with the woman he had made love to, so tenderly, just hours ago. "Rose, I'm so sorry. You know how much I love you." His eyes finally caught mine. Tears rolled down my face and fell on the papers in my hand. Clay blinked his tears away, apparently not wanting to cry in front of the deputy.

"This isn't my place to say this, but," Deputy Bryant broke the silence, "Something isn't right here. If you two are supposed to be a divorcing couple, you certainly aren't talking like one."

"You're right, deputy, we're in love," I said, not taking my eyes off that beautiful face that I had fallen in love with so many years ago.

Clay took off his Stetson and ran his tanned fingers through that famous mop of hair which had now had more salt than pepper woven through it. He was still my beautiful man. My handsome prince who I thought was going to keep me safe, slay my dragons, and sweep me off to his castle for our happy ending.

Here in this kitchen, as the ingredients for our island dinner turned rancid in the car, I was facing a different ending to my fairy tale. Apparently, my knight in shining armor couldn't scrape up the courage to kick his siblings' butts and save our marriage. He's a coward and he has caved. He has given in to the demands of that wicked, hateful family of his and I'm being tossed aside.

"She's right, deputy, I love her, but we just can't be together. We have our reasons." With that, Clay put on his hat, walked out the door, and drove away.

I watched as the taillights disappeared over the hill down on the highway. My cowboy was riding into the sunset. Without me.

"Officer, I stood up to his meddling family and they did this. They had these papers drawn up while we were on vacation. Clay had nothing to do with this. He's just going along with it to please them! He doesn't want a divorce—it's just that he can't stand up to his family."

I don't know what kept the deputy from roaring with laughter over my childish denial. He swiftly flipped through the papers and pointed to Clay's signature. The papers were signed and dated exactly one week before we left to go on vacation. *One week* before!

"My husband is a coward," I said. I was vacillating between confusion and anger, but I was finally coming to grips with the truth that had been staring me in the face for years.

"Well, Mrs. Hutchison, I'm not rushing you or anything, but I'm supposed to stay here until you gather your belongings and leave," Deputy Bryant cleared his throat and looked through the stack of papers again to find a ridiculous restraining order, throwing me off the property until a hearing before a judge. It, too, had been signed by Clay on the same day.

"Get my belongings!? And do what? And go where? Does it say what the hell I'm supposed to do exactly?" I was raising my voice at this poor kid who was just the messenger.

"Yes, Mrs. Hutchison, just gather a few personal items of clothing you'll need until the settlement is final. The judge will set a date when you will be escorted back here to move."

From that moment on, I remember events only in a fog—kind of like a dream you have when you're running a fever, a fitful, sleepless night of disturbing thoughts constantly running through your head. I walked back to the bedroom in that foggy state. I didn't know where to begin, so I grabbed my still-unpacked suitcase from our vacation. I didn't stop to think about what I might need to wear in this chilly fall weather. I didn't consider the contents of the suitcase: a makeup kit, two dirty swimsuits, some underwear, T-shirts and shorts, a couple of pairs of thin sweat pants and a souvenir sweatshirt from Little Palm Island.

I didn't have the wherewithal to put an appropriate outfit together or to pack a coat, shoes, toothpaste, little things that we take for granted, little things homeless people hoard like gold. I was about to join their ranks in approximately one hour. For the first time in my 58 years on the earth, I had absolutely no where to go. My sister and her teenaged daughter now occupied my home.

There was no room for me and I couldn't ask them to leave. I didn't have enough money in my savings account for a down payment on another home and I certainly wouldn't qualify for a mortgage with no income at my age. I had no furniture for an apartment. No bed. Not even a chair to my name. Perhaps my sister would be kind enough to allow me to sleep on her couch. That would have to be my refuge until I could think—until I could wake up from this nightmare and figure out what had just happened to me. The deputy watched from the kitchen door as I walked down the hall with my suitcase. All the while, my mind was reeling. Here comes the bag lady. Look at the tanned, well-dressed bag lady—fresh from her island vacation. My, she certainly has a nice haircut for someone who lives on the street!

As I walked out to the car with my bags, I remembered the groceries. I would have to take them with me. I didn't want to walk into my sister's home empty-handed and I could at least cook a nice dinner for them before I crashed on their sofa. As for me, I may never eat again. Food would only taste like wallpaper paste to me from now on. I popped the trunk lid and was stuffing my luggage between the grocery bags when it occurred to me that this wasn't even my car. This ten year old Ford Taurus belonged to Hutchison Farms. I sold my little Toyota when I quit work and Clay wanted me to drive this big car when I went to Lafayette because it was sturdy and safe. It never occurred to me that I would have to worry about a vehicle ever again. Clay always took care of the cars, the upkeep and the tires. I've worked in factories all my life, even for half of this marriage to help Clay. I've waited tables to help my family, I've saved my money and shown other people how to cut corners and save their money. Why has it ended like this? As of this moment, I have no husband, no home, no job, no car, and no life for that matter. My independence was gone and so, now, was the love of my life.

All I had left were questions and no one—not even the coward who filed for the divorce and threw me out on my ear—had the answers. The deputy was patient enough to help me into the car with his condolences. He was still shaking his head, not completely understanding what he had just witnessed. He told me to call the number at the bottom of the cover page in the documents and the attorney's office would let me know when I could come back for the rest of my personal belongings.

"I'm really sorry, Mrs. Hutchison. This is the part of my job that I really don't like."

"You're simply doing what you must, deputy. Thank you for being so kind." I had to close the door and leave before I broke down. I felt a crying jag coming on and I didn't want to lose it in front of this young deputy who had already blown his entire afternoon dealing with this crazy Hutchison clan.

The engine of the car was still warm from my trip to Lafayette. Less than an hour ago, I had spotted that deputy's cruiser and had driven up this winding road in a different frame of mind entirely—thinking that my love might be hurt, fearing that he could have been in an accident and that I may never see him again. I was terrified when I parked this car. Now, I'm driving back down the driveway and I'm still terrified. The result is the same. I *have* lost my husband. Not to a drunk driver or faulty tractor brakes, but to his greedy, cruel, insane family. This time, when the Hutchison compound is in my rear-view mirror, it could very well be the last chance I have to see it as "Mrs. Clay Hutchison."

So, I chose not to look back at all. I looked straight ahead at the road in front of me.

Sis, I'm home!

My sister Joan and her daughter, Sandy were just getting home from a shopping trip when, for the second time that day, I pulled into the driveway of my familiar little cottage in Lafayette. They stopped at the foot of the front steps and were obviously surprised to see me again. It only took one look at my face for Joan to realize something was terribly wrong. We embraced.

"Clay chose his family over me, Sis!" Even I was shocked at the first thing that came out of my mouth. We held each other without saying a word. That's what sisters do. Then, without missing a beat, we unloaded groceries, removed my luggage, and put everything away. I would be staying in the room with my niece for the time being.

It felt so odd to be back at this house. It was as though time had stood still. Joan left all the furniture arranged just as I had it—the same drapes, shades, rugs. It was in this living room that I had married Clay. I was lying on that sofa when mama answered the phone the night he called and asked me out on our first date. I found myself wondering—if I had a time machine, would I go back and do it all again? Is there anything I would do differently? What horrible sin had I committed to have it all end this way?

Joan insisted on preparing dinner for the three of us, but I couldn't eat a bite. They ate on TV trays in the living room while watching a movie and I paced the hallway.

Back and forth, up and down. I couldn't sit still. I wanted to take action. I wanted to do something—or I wanted someone to do something on my behalf to stop this court action before it went any further. I wanted to talk to Clay without a deputy standing beside me holding divorce papers and a restraining order, but there was nothing I could do tonight.

It was the weekend and I wouldn't be able to do anything tomorrow either. My heart was pounding out of my chest and I was shaking. Joan came out to the hallway to check on me now and then, asking me if I wanted to talk, asking me if I needed anything. I could tell she was starting to worry, so I went back to my niece's bedroom and sat at her desk in the dark, staring out the window at the streetlights in my familiar old neighborhood, trying not to make a nuisance of myself.

Sandy sauntered in after watching a movie and was ready to crash for the night but I couldn't imagine climbing into the other little twin bed and lying still until morning. The thought of being there at that moment and looking at that possibility made me cry. Sandy stood over me, held my head against her stomach, and rocked me like a child. Joan rushed in with a glass of warm milk and one of her sleeping pills, but I didn't want to sleep. I wanted to talk. My precious sis and my sweet niece sat on the edge of the bed as I recounted the entire afternoon and the disturbing details leading up to it. They listened with open hearts and mouths as I gave them a play-by-play of perverted old Bernard, Therlow and his threats, Rena and her madness.

It was cathartic to get this all out in the open to my sister who dearly loves me and my teenaged niece, who was just beginning to learn the ways of romance. It did a world of good to have someone mirror the shock and disgust at what I had been through. Clay had never done that. Whenever I would be upset about something his family had done to hurt me, Clay would remain calm and stare straight ahead. No emotion, no shock, no empathy. What a relief to come home and have someone on my side!

By 2AM, I could tell our little slumber party was winding down. Sandy and Joan could barely keep their eyes open and I was starting to repeat myself. I continued to ask over and over "Why? Why does he want a divorce if he loves me?" I kissed both of them goodnight, but I knew I couldn't sleep in that quiet house. Talking about all of this had given me a second wind. I went out for a drive.

Lost In Lafayette

Lafayette had changed quite a bit since I lived here. There was a new park with pavilions and a jogging trail across from what used to be Cothron Chevrolet. I almost got lost as I tried to maneuver around the recently completed bypass. On my shopping trips here, I never ventured out beyond the beauty shop and grocery store. I was always in a hurry to get home to Clay.

Riding up to the square and the courthouse, I parked in front of the building where City Café used to be. Suddenly, it hit me that things can change *forever* in the wink of an eye. When I was little, I thought this town would always look like it did back then—two five and dimes, three or four dry goods stores, a fabric shop, two drug stores, two hardware stores and even a shoe store.

Now, every storefront was different—some were empty. Nothing was the way it had been when City Café was here beside Trapp Jewelers. Lafayette Dry Goods was gone. McClard's Drugs was closed, the owners long since retired.

After the café closed, Highland Appliance was the place where everyone gathered to socialize and catch up on the news. Now, even that huge presence on the corner was abandoned, the shades drawn over dusty plate-glass windows. I used to go in to Ben Franklin's 5&10 to buy my little brothers and sisters their favorite candy on payday. I can still smell the hot cashews roasting in the display case at the front door. There's a flower shop in that store now.

This trip down memory lane was taking me into the deep recesses of my mind. It was transporting me to such a happy time in my life when my precious parents were alive, I had a job I loved and friends I adored. I was as poor as a church mouse, but so rich in spirit and so full of promise.

I was never lonely when I came to the square here in Lafayette. There was always something going on and I knew everyone I passed on the street. They certainly don't make towns like this anymore—towns where kids can grow up feeling special. Growing up here and walking around this quaint little square, I had the feeling that everybody knew my name and cared about my welfare. They knew my parents, my brothers and sisters, and they were always so kind to wish me a good day and give me a smile.

What I would give to wake up tomorrow morning and find it all here again, just as it was back then! I wanted to go back to a time when I didn't know Clay and didn't care—back to a time when I had wonderful possibilities and miles and miles of a bright future stretched out in front of me.

Looking back at happier times for those few moments was just what I needed, but I had to snap out of it. Back to reality. In less than eight years, I'll be on Social Security. There isn't much time left. There certainly isn't a lot of time for me to assess what I want to do with the rest of my life, what road I might choose, what career skills I might want to learn. I am a 58 year old woman who was just turned out to pasture by a man who had promised to love me forever. I'm sitting here with photographs of my belated honeymoon in my purse, a dark tan from the island, and a broken heart.

I started the car and I don't even remember how I got there, but I do remember why I wanted to go; I wanted to be close to the two people who always made me feel better when I was hurting. I drove to the cemetery. I knelt beside the headstones of my mama and daddy and "talked" to them about the only man I had ever loved—the only man who had ever truly loved me. I prayed for guidance and, for a moment, I prayed that God would see fit to let me join my parents very soon. I was so weary. I needed rest and I needed *peace*. It seemed I had not had one minute of that precious commodity since I married Clay and my thought processes were turning toward the easy way out. And why not? Clay had certainly chosen his easiest way. I walked back to the car, exhausted from praying and bone-tired from driving. I stretched out in the front seat and slept there, parked in the cemetery, until the sun rose.

It gets worse.......

Monday came and I was eager to call the attorney and find out what was going on and what I was supposed to do while I awaited this hearing the deputy had talked about. The restraining order made no sense. After all, don't people get those when they're concerned for their safety? I wouldn't hurt Clay. I should have been the one to get a restraining order against Therlow, since he had threatened me and put his fist in my face. The hearing was to be held the following month and according to the order, I had to wait until then to gather the rest of my belongings from Clay's house. That wasn't acceptable.

I waited until around noon to call Clay. I knew he would be in the house having his lunch and his midday nap and would be alone. He didn't have Caller I.D. Not many people did out in the country, so he answered the phone.

I put on my best business-like demeanor and was determined to stick to the unemotional subject of picking up my belongings. He seemed genuinely happy that I called. I got right to it. I told him I had left in such a hurry that I didn't have the proper clothing for the cold weather and I needed some sweaters, jeans, and jackets. Without hesitation, he told me he would have some of my things packed and ready to be picked up by the afternoon. There was something in his voice that seemed so relieved to hear from me. I was getting the idea that maybe he had spent the weekend in that lonely old house and had thought better of this ridiculous notion of throwing his wife out to make room for his wicked siblings and their spouses.

For some strange reason, I experienced a panic attack as I showered and dressed, but the long drive from Lafayette gave me time to calm down and muster up the courage to do what must be done. I couldn't show up on his doorstep a sniveling, sobbing wreck. I needed to act like a queen; a very pissed-off queen, from whose good graces he had fallen drastically.

I drove up the long, winding driveway and didn't see cars at the other houses, but Clay's pick-up was in the garage and the door was up. Two big boxes were stacked on the porch. I rang the bell and Clay cracked open the door to reveal only half his face.

"Hello, my love," he whispered as though he feared someone was listening in. "Your clothes are right there in those boxes," he continued and gestured with one of his fingers through the crack.

"Okay," I said as I looked at the boxes—sizing them up and trying to decide if they would fit better in the trunk or the back seat. I tried to lift one, but the dead weight kept me from budging it one inch.

"Clay... could.... you.... help... me?" I grunted through clinched teeth as I tried to scoot the hefty box down the steps with my foot.

"Hon, I'd better not. Try to drag it," he said. I couldn't believe what I was hearing.

Clay stood there with the door open only about an inch and watched me wrestle both boxes into the trunk.

"Hon, can you stay and talk a while?"

I thought with that invitation, he'd open the door and we would sit in the living room and have a discussion like two adults. No such luck. I walked up to the door and tried to get close enough to see more than one eye. It's difficult to carry on a conversation with someone's left eye.

"How have you been, my love?" Clay asked as though nothing out of the ordinary had happened in our relationship in the past few days.

"Not so good, Clay. This is like a bad dream. What is your problem? Why won't you ask me in?"

"No can do, Rose. I can't explain it right now, but I just can't let you in this house. Are you cold, my love?" With that, he opened the door about a foot and began to "fan" the heat outside to me as he attempted to carry on a conversation.

"I've missed you. It's not the same in this house without my Rose," he said, as he continued to wave the heat out to me with a folded newspaper. His voice had a different tone—a Peter Lorre quality to it that gave me the creeps.

"Clay, I just don't understand. If we can sit down and talk about this, we'll work things out. Why are you acting this way?" I was frustrated, I was cold, and he was trying my patience.

"You know I love you, Rose," he whispered.

"If you loved me, you wouldn't treat me this way, Clay! Why are you asking for a divorce?"

Before he could answer, Therlow drove up, brought his truck to a screeching halt, and rolled down the window.

"Bitch, get off 'at porch! You ain't supposed to be here! Get off this prop'etee right now or I'm gonna come up thar 'n take care 'a you myself!" Therlow squealed the tires as he drove to his house and sat in the driveway, revving the motor as if to send me the message that he wasn't joking about taking care of me for good. He was slumped over and seemed to be searching for something in the glove compartment of his truck. I don't know if he was going to pull out a gun or a monkey wrench. Either way, I do believe he would have hurt me—or worse if I had not left at that moment.

Clay didn't say a word, but quickly slammed the door in my face once he saw Therlow. I jogged off the porch under Therlow's watchful eye and drove away, leaving the Hutchison compound, yet again, with a horrible feeling in the pit of my stomach. I would know better than to do this again. What was I *thinking*?

That night, as I lay on my sister's sofa, I couldn't stop crying. The hurt was piling on and I was inconsolable. I was sad, then, I was angry. Then, one minute later, I wouldn't know what to call the emotion. I cried until I developed the dry heaves. Sis had put up with this long enough. She couldn't bear to see me waste away before her very eyes.

Sis took me to the emergency room that night, but I've already told you about that experience.....

The Hits Keep Coming

Once I was released from the hospital, I came back to the cottage and my Sis, but I knew I couldn't stay there. This was now her home and I was an intruder. I felt I didn't fit in anywhere. I was no longer anyone's employee. I was no longer a homemaker—no one's daughter, no one's mother, no one's wife. I was just another over-fifty woman who had fallen off the horse and I didn't know the first thing about getting back in the saddle. Nor did I want to.

I apparently knew even less about the divorce process. I squeezed out the bare minimum in the settlement; leaving this nightmare with far less than I had coming into it. After sixteen years of marriage to a man owning property worth more than 2.5 million dollars, I limped away with practically zip. I ended up with my clothing and what I would have in the bank if I had never met Clay, worked at the factory, and saved my money for as little as four years.

I moved into low-income housing for a while as I got my bearings. It's all I could afford. What was so painful about that experience was learning that Clay couldn't have cared less about my struggle. He was only concerned with continuing the fantasy—training me like Pavlov's dog to answer the phone any time he felt like whispering sweet, long-distance nothings into a cold, plastic receiver.

Onward!

Luckily, several years out from that horrible experience, I was able to re-invent myself career wise and I think that's the hardest part of divorce for any woman my age. I became a home caregiver to a sweet elderly couple and this has helped tremendously in my complicated healing process. They treat me as loving parents would and I adore them. I stay active and involved with this energetic couple—I'm not as self-absorbed. That's a vital part of healing and finding life worth living again. I do understand now that finding happiness within is a long journey and there are no shortcuts. I've never spent a great deal of time alone. Before I married Clay, I lived in my house with my sister and before she moved in, there was Mama. There was always someone to come home to, someone who was worried about me when I was sick. There was always someone to share my day and my stories with. Now I didn't fit in. Life had gone forward, people had paired off and I was single again. Following the divorce I had to re-learn living. Where do I begin? How do I begin? They don't teach classes in "Senior Divorce Survival."

If I were in my twenties or thirties, I'd probably grab my best gal friends and we would be off to the Titan's game, tailgating. We would check out the crowd at "The Palm," or listen to some music at the Bluebird Café or at the symphony hall.

Oh the things I could do to get over this divorce if I were younger!

At my age, when you've lived the quiet, proper life of a small town southern lady for so long, it's a tad jolting to the system to be forced into the social scene and boldly go where the action is.

I don't want to be where the action is. If something exciting is going on down the street, I hope no one calls me.

When I was an "old maid," I was content. I could have gone on living that life forever. But I've been married to the love of my life for the past sixteen years. I'm used to seeing his face every morning at breakfast—having lunch with him and lying beside him for his midday nap. When he sneezed, I was standing there holding a tissue. How do you go from that kind of togetherness to nothing without feeling a gaping hole in your heart?

I've talked this through with counselors enough to know that I can't rush the healing. The healing will come—but I learned the hard way that I simply cannot continue to rip the scab off this open wound. After the divorce was final, Clay continued to call. I should not have allowed it. To my detriment, we spent hours talking about our love, our life together, how we met and our wonderful island vacation. Noticeably absent from our conversation was why we divorced and why he didn't love me enough to stand up for us against his family. He told me how much he loved me each time we talked. I told him that I never stopped loving him. After each marathon conversation, I would spend the next day in a deep depression, crying, aching for Clay, wanting our life together. It was torture.

The Last Straw

In a weak moment, only a year after the divorce was final, I drove to the Hutchison compound at Clay's invitation. Clay said he wanted to talk about something very important and it had to be face to face. This time, he promised he would sit on the front porch with me instead of speaking through a crack in the door. I thought he had finally grown a pair, but upon my arrival at the compound, I learned his siblings were on vacation in Europe. That explained this sudden bout of courage. I'm sure their trip was bankrolled with my blood-money; the money Bernard had left them if they were successful in getting me out of the family.

We sat on the wicker sofa out on the veranda and as we talked and kissed, he laid his head in my lap, an old habit from our lazy Sunday afternoons in the summer. There were few words between us, but unlike those endless first dates of enduring Clay's shyness, this was a comfortable, restful quiet.

He broke the silence by proposing an unusual scenario that, looking back today, reeked of a set up. He asked if I would consider marrying him *again* if we could live somewhere—anywhere else but here in the compound. Then, he said he had a surprise for me that he had been waiting to share for a long time. He told me that his siblings would not get their way when he died after all; he was hinting—ever so cleverly—that in a fit of spite he had changed his will, leaving everything to *me*.

I don't know what kind of reaction he expected but the mere thought of getting into that Vietnam again made me squirm. I was thinking 'there he goes down that road again' talking as if he were at death's door. It all came rushing back to me, the cause of all our problems in the first place. Clay was as obsessed as his siblings with death, control, money—*material things*.

At that instant, Clay grabbed his chest and gasped for breath. His face turned red and enlarged veins became visible on his neck and temples. Then, it appeared he stopped breathing. My love was having a heart attack!

I scrambled off the sofa and got to work with everything I learned in CPR class. As he gasped, I checked his mouth for obstructions and began chest compressions—all the while, trying to think how I could get to the phone in the living room and keep him breathing until the paramedics got there. I decided to make my move. I dragged the limp and seemingly unconscious Clay as close to the front door as possible while continuing the chest compressions. I told him through my tears to hang in there, that I loved him, and that I was running to the living room to call 911.

As I stood to head for the door, Clay sat up, perfectly calm, and broke into roaring laughter. He laughed so hard that he began to cough and it reminded me of Bernard so long ago after the awful fondling incident. It turned my stomach.

"That was a test, Rosie! I was wonderin' if you would try to save me or let me die after you found out that I willed everything to you," he could barely get the words out as he climbed onto the sofa, still laughing uncontrollably and wiping the tears rolling down his cheeks. "Aw, honey! This proves that you love me, don't you see? It proves that you love me no matter what," Clay managed to calm his laughter and put on a more serious demeanor. "It means our love is true. I wish you could have seen the look on your face!"

I was livid. I've never been more incensed or felt more absolute contempt for any human being in my life. How could he do this to me? He had finally lost it.

"You bastard! You sick, twisted, bastard!" I screamed, as I stared him down and slammed the front door with all the strength I could muster. I was off the porch and in my car within seconds.

"You self-centered, conceited, materialistic, bastard! Do *not* call me, do *not* attempt to visit. I never want to hear from you or see you again as long as I live." I started the engine and was squealing tires as I burned rubber down the driveway of the Hutchison compound for the last time. Finally, after all these years and all this pain and abuse I had been thumped on the head one too many times. At long last.

That did it for me. This crazy incident was all I needed to decide that this man was a card-carrying lunatic who would never leave his family, never quite give up being "Little Clay" there on the big Ponderosa they call the Hutchison Compound. It forced me to see that all along, Clay was every bit as disturbed and mentally off-kilter as the rest of his family, but his illness had simply manifested itself in a different way. I had to think of Clay as dead—buried. The fantasy had died. In every way I became a widow that day.

Realizing he had lost me for good after a few days, Clay panicked and began to call my relatives weekly—asking about my well-being, my social life, and my whereabouts. These calls continued for several months until everyone stopped answering the phone whenever they saw his number on Caller I.D.

Today, as I work toward getting my life back, I think the fever has finally broken. I still cry when I talk to people about my experiences, but the tears aren't for Clay. They are for me and the memory of my horrible pain. The tears are for the emotional abuse and disrespect I suffered while living at the Hutchison compound.

Mostly, I cry for lost years and true love that might have been—true love I might have found with someone normal had I not wasted the best years of my life with Clay.

I feel sorry for Clay because he lives in a self-imposed prison. I worry about his wasted life and I wish he would seek counseling for the deep emotional problems he's harbored for so many years. I can't turn off my love for him as I turn off the water faucet, but I can certainly change that love into pity. I do pity him.

I also worry about his physical well-being. If his siblings are so concerned about his last will and testament, how far would they go to see to it that he "goes" first? Clay told me shortly after the divorce was final that he feared his sister would have him "put away," and deemed incompetent to handle his affairs. I don't know why he continues to live with fear like that. I'm glad I'm out of there.

It could have been so wonderful, but I've learned that I fell in love with a fantasy. The reality was the hell that I lived through. But I did "live to tell about it," as my daddy used to say. I pray that by living through it and choosing to tell you about the experience, that the story will help save you or a loved one from the immeasurable pain of emotional abuse that bruises the spirit and wounds the soul.

I pray that unlike me, you'll recognize the early warning signs in those who are incapable of love; the sadists who have been damaged by their childhood almost beyond repair. I don't know about you, but I'm not in the business of attempting those repairs. There are licensed professionals who do a very good job of putting Humpty-Dumpty back together again and I hope Clay will consult with someone who can help him. I don't have the inclination nor would I even know where to begin with him. My energy must be spent putting my own life back in order.

I *do* know that, perhaps, I've been pruned to bloom. Someday, I'll be a beautiful Rose once again, but these things take time. I have plenty of that. Meanwhile, I'll surround myself with positive people who feed my soul, renew my spirit, and remind me that my sunniest days are still ahead here where I began, and where I am blessed, in lovely little Lafayette, Tennessee.

Love and Peace to you,

Epilogue

Every day, it's getting easier. I'm finding that I can forgive Clay and his strange family as time goes by, and most importantly, I've finally forgiven myself for overlooking some pretty obvious signs that he wasn't in any position to form a healthy relationship. I almost have my life back and I'm to the point where I'm getting out socially—meeting friends for dinner and going to cocktail parties. Walking in the door to these social gatherings without a man on my arm took some getting used to, but I'm doing it. I'm holding my head up high and I'm getting better at faking my confidence until I actually feel comfortable about being on my own again.

Recently, my friend Sara invited me to a spring cookout at her house and I was surprised to see a patio full of single, over-fifty men and women who were all apparently in the same boat. They were now alone due to a divorce or the death of their spouse (practically the same things in my experience). I scanned the crowd for familiar faces, but before I could make my way to where some ladies from my school days were gathered, a handsome, nicely dressed gentleman with slightly graying hair and horn-rimmed glasses approached me. Something about him screamed intelligence. After what I'd been through, this was refreshing.

"Are you Roseleen?" he asked with a hint of a British accent. It startled me, since no one since grade school has called me by that name.

"Why, yes! How did you know my full name? Are you from Lafayette?" I smiled as I tried to figure out how he could possible know me.

"No, we haven't met, but Sara and I work together. She speaks of you highly as one of her dear friends and asked me to come over and introduce myself. I'm Brad Rainey, by the way."

This man had a kind demeanor and I was impressed that he had the courage to boldly approach me in this room full of strangers. As we talked, we made our way to the buffet tables to fill our plates and I introduced him to the few people that I knew there. For me, it was like old home week, but he had just been transferred to Franklin from the New York office to run the computer software company and he didn't know anyone. I could tell he was grateful that I was helping him work through the crowd. We found a comfortable wicker sofa on the patio overlooking a sparkling pool and the bed of Sara's award-winning roses which were starting to bud. Brad brought us two glasses of red wine from the bar and sat beside me, holding his glass in front of him as if preparing to make a toast. The sun was beginning to set and the warm, spring breeze smelled so sweet. I took a deep breath. For the first time in a long while, it felt good to be alive and out and about with a group people who not only seemed happy to see me, but seemed genuinely interested in what I had to say. What a departure!

"By the way, Brad, do you have any brothers or sisters?" I asked.

"No, Rose, I'm afraid I'm an only child. All alone in this world."

"Thank you Jesus!" I said, as I looked up to the sky and laughed.

"To new friends!" Brad held his glass to mine with a puzzled look on his face.

"To new friends!" I said, as we clicked glasses and took our first sip of wine.

AFTERWORD

Help, Health, and Healing

for the Emotionally Abused Woman

By *Susan Gillpatrick, LPC, CTS, CEAP*

From playing spin the bottle to spinning her wheels trying to just be an accepted part of her new family, the story of Rose and the "thorns" she endured, offers us many lessons on relationship dynamics—mostly lessons about those unhealthy little toxins that seem to creep in, and the wishing and hoping and dreaming that they weren't there. Clearly, there were issues concerning denial, boundaries, relationship red flags, codependence, emotional abuse and more.

In this Afterword, I will offer some advice for identifying those unhealthy patterns, and suggestions for recovery, resiliency and strength. I will detail seven tips you can integrate into your life today, inspired by the courageous story shared by Rose. You will see how there can be good news about stress. You just need to take that first step forward. There is life after abuse, disappointment, disrespect and divorce.

As the story began, Rose was a shining example of a secure, stable and independent young woman. She enjoyed the simple abundance of catering to caring customers in her job as a waitress. She supported herself. She came from a humble background. She didn't need material things to feel success. She knew the difference in needs and wants. In Rose's teen years she had supportive friends—friends who "had her back"—a quality that was glaringly absent in her marriage. She had friends who would keep her secrets, unlike her husband who kept secrets from her.

When her cherished City Café job came to an end, Rose was assertive in seeking new work. She was not passive and just hoping something would change—very unlike the passivity that framed her future marriage. More on this later...

The lure of his turquoise eyes led to many miles together back and forth to Ponderosa for Clay and Rose, but she eventually became hungry for more than steak and potatoes. She wanted connection, sharing, and an adult relationship. Rose was eager to learn about Clay and wanted Clay to want to learn about her. She could see the disengagement in their relationship on their first date—but why couldn't she so clearly visualize that same disconnect in their future home when she was slicing, dicing, baking and roasting every day? And when she did finally see it, she refused to stand up for herself—refused to hold Clay accountable for his corrupt family. More on these relationship red flags in the following pages.

In her dating years Rose knew what she wouldn't settle for. She was not a mission to be married, so she was discerning in her relationships. She refused to take on other peoples' crap, so to speak. She knew many men came with a boatload of baggage she didn't want to tote. So why did she tote so much family friction baggage with

Afterword

Clay? When did she loose her inner voice, her intuition? What took her so long so speak up and demand support and understanding? If you were like me, in reading her story, you also wanted to yell out, "*Say something!*" to Rose, as she was being slowly corralled by Clay's clan. But she just took it…for a while.

Rose was long in patience with Clay. I suggest *too* long. She would distract herself in lavender baths to wash away her disappointments while they dated. She enjoyed catering to his needs, and asked little in return. She was fully cognizant he was offering little more than consistent boredom in the beginning. Yet she kept herself attached to a man who had his attachments elsewhere—his farm and his family. Even when she courageously told him they were going in opposite directions, that purposeful boundary of the break up only lasted a year.

Rides in a shiny new pick up and Clay's improved communication skills soon led to Rose professing her love. She fell for him. She needed him. And some part of her knew he was too good to be true. I think, as many women tend to do, she minimized those doubts and just focused on the "good signs". When someone shows us who they are, we should listen the *first* time. There may be plenty of good pieces of the relationship, but never assume someone will change just because of love.

A *decade* later—indeed not the speed of romance in a Lifetime movie—ten full years of togetherness without meeting Clay's family, a family Rose knew was alive and thriving on a ranch not too far away. Sometimes the power of being in love blinds one to the beaming red flags. Why wasn't he proud to show-off his lady love prior to pinning her down with a ring? Why wasn't she insistent he bring her out from hiding? This is a hallmark sign of emotional abuse—the control and manipulation masked in secrecy and coated in chocolates.

Rose did not likely envision living in a "lion's den" as newlywed. I think she became codependent with Clay, living on those three words "I love you" to mask the ongoing unhealthy patterns with her new in-laws. Unhealthy relationships are a dangerous thing because they don't have to be gritty, dirty and filled with physical punches to scar the people who get caught up in them. Rose got caught up accepting the emotional abuse of Clay and his family. She chose to take the blows of verbal putdowns, manipulation and lies, without requiring her dear Clay to stand up and be a real man. Clay acted like a bystander, just new to town, not knowing anyone. But he was her "wonderful Clay". She was his first and only girlfriend. So wasn't that enough, she likely thought?

Rose admitted she rationalized the red flag of Clay not wanting any of his family at their wedding. How she took that as "not her business" escapes me. After all, she would have her family there. She also just swallowed her hometown hubby's plan of living with a more-than-grouchy old man, her father-in-law. She catered to the whole family, with the same reliability she did at the City Café. But now, she didn't receive tips or appreciation for sharing her homemaker passions. She bent over backwards to meet everyone's needs—yet another sign of

Afterword

poor boundaries. One-way relationship accommodation means someone is being used.

Rose chose to let Clay's sweet words wash off the hateful remarks from his family. She was not aggressive or assertive in claiming her right to be respected. And just when she thought she had all she could take, she finally broke her silence. Her knight in shining armor simply suggested she "sleep in" the next morning. With no evidence thus far, Rose naively believed Clay would sprint to defend her. I'm glad she is not still waiting...

One of Rose's most passive habits was not holding Clay accountable. She required no follow up from her requests or his from his promises. Even when she was emotionally and mentally beaten down, sobbing in Clay's arms, he brushed her off suggesting she see a doctor. I bet she felt she *was* going crazy at that point. She was practically all alone emotionally, yet surrounded by a cult-like environment. She continued to take darts to the heart from each of Clay's family members.

Clay even couched her very valid complaints with his idea of a trip. I suppose he thought sweeping her away to an island would effortlessly delete the problems. After all, he thought, the problems were all in *her* head. He had no problem.

Rose never asked for a trip or to be a beneficiary of a will. She meekly longed for her husband to understand and support her. But Clay bailed on the "Butting Out 101" intervention. His family enmeshment was too deep and too powerful. Those bonds could not and would not be broken.

There are only so many sunflower bundles and "sweetheart" words that can accompany excuses and make them acceptable.

The "perfect honeymoon" came without yet another promise being realized. I almost tossed this book across the room when I read Rose went on the trip without any discussion of Clay attempting to "call his family on the carpet", as we say in the South. I could almost see the denial fill the airplane as it headed to Key West, like thick, black smog. After all, drinks with little umbrellas and tropical sunsets make for ideal blinders of wrecked relationship realities. Although Rose's rosy glasses (with Clay's strategic diversions) did a great job in keeping things afloat, it appeared her (caged) needs back in Kentucky were a faint memory. Honeymoons don't last forever.

Back home, the euphoric mood that accompanied the Jimmy Buffet tunes was quickly subdued when Rose was served papers by the deputy, but her illusion of an innocent spouse still stood strong. Clay's claims he "didn't know what else to do" and his "bravely blinked tears" were still not a wakeup call that her days as Mrs. Clay Hutchison were numbered.

The proverbial stack of straws must have filled the Grand Canyon before Rose tripped onto *her* "last straw". When she accepted being (emotionally) being kicked to the curb, I feared nothing would be her last straw.

Afterword

Sometimes we have to learn the lesson over and over before we accept the realities. We want to believe in the best of others. We live safely in our fantasies. We believe people will change just because they say the love us. Rose never wanted to give up. There was enough "good" in the relationship, she settled for so much bad—until realities overwhelmed not just her mind, but her body.

The psychological wounding she endured finally got the best of her. Her sister's sofa was not enough solace to recover on her own. A sixteen year marriage which included daily lunches with her beloved was a history too hard to erase on her own. It makes sense that Rose would still ache for a new life with Clay, even though she was surrounded in depression. She had years of momentum from hiding in her happy thoughts and minimizing her frustrations.

Rose was too sweet, too trusting. She was humble and giving. She even thanked the deputy for his patience, just minutes before she was escorted from her own home. And she wasn't skilled at "playing pissed off" or playing a "Queen". Therlow was King and Commander now. Clay kept his puppet suit donned and remained fully submitted to the Hutchison plan to keep Rose out.

There were no magic pills at the hospital to minimize her deep emotional pain. And it was not just a nightmare that Clay faked a heart attack. It was real—real trickery, devious and deliberate. After many tears and realizing valuable years were lost, Rose *did* survive! She resumed her life in Lafayette. She was able to reframe her view of her past sick "family". She was able to separate from the dysfunction. She was able to remove the delusions that Clay would somehow wake up and be a different man. I champion her resiliency! Rose is working on reinventing herself. Life is never too short to make a new and improved decision.

No matter our age, our status, or what we don't have, our greatness is still there. Remember, we can't change somebody else no matter how hard we try if they are not willing to change. That's why we could always start by changing ourselves first and maybe the rest will come naturally. Maya Angelou said, "There is **no agony** like bearing an untold story inside of you." The story of Rose has been told and we should be grateful. In the following pages, I'll offer seven suggestions to maximize an emotionally healthy life! The tips are inspired by the lessons learned in *Thorns on the Rose*. They include:

1. Signs of toxic relationship
2. How to communicate through conflict
3. Love is caring—not controlling
4. Six simple secrets of great relationships
5. Self-care strategies for women
6. How to know when it is time to seek counseling
7. The good news about stress

Afterword

1. The Toxic Relationship

If you allow them, toxic people can be like vampires—draining your energy mentally, emotionally, and financially. When you are with them your mood sours and you struggle to be at your best. To sum it up, after you've been with a toxic person(s) you feel the need to shower yourself in some positivity. The Hutchison clan reeked toxicity. Do any of these sound familiar in any of your relationships?

Signs of a toxic relationship:

- It brings out the worst in you rather than your best.
- You put much more into the relationship than you ever get out of it.
- One person gives up his or her own values and dreams to satisfy the other person. You should not have to betray yourself by setting your dreams aside for another person. That puts the relationship out of balance and infers that one person is more important than the other. When we betray our dreams and values, we betray ourselves.
- You spend all your time with only that person to the exclusion of all other friends.
- When one person becomes what he/she thinks the other wants him/her to be rather than expressing himself/herself honestly.
- Going against your better judgment and gut instinct, due to intrigue and mystery.
- Constant sarcasm, put downs, or "just joking".

- When you're working so hard to please and nothing seems to work.
- Bad boundaries—when you feel you have no "voice" to say "no" or anything.

Someone once said,
"If you don't feel like being a door mat, get off the floor".

When you give up your boundaries in a relationship you:
- Do not notice unhappiness since simply enduring is your concern
- Alter your behavior, plans, or opinions to fit the current moods or circumstances of another (live reactively)
- Do more and more for less and less
- Take as truth the most recent opinion you have heard
- Live hopefully while wishing and waiting
- Are satisfied if you are coping and surviving
- Let the other's minimal improvement maintain your stalemate
- Are manipulated by flattery so you lose objectivity
- Will forsake every personal limit to get affection or the promise of it
- See your partner as causing your excitement
- Feel hurt and victimized but not angry
- Act out of compliance and compromise
- Disregard intuition in favor of wishes
- Allow your partner (or their family or friends) to intimidate you

- Mostly feel afraid and confused
- Are enmeshed in a drama that is beyond your control
- Are living a life that is not yours, and that seems unalterable
- Commit yourself for as long as the other needs you to be committed (no bottom line)

When your boundaries are intact in a relationship you:
- Have clear preferences and act upon them
- Recognize when you are happy/unhappy
- Trust your own intuition while being open to other's opinions
- Live optimistically while co-working on change
- Are only satisfied if you are thriving
- Are encouraged by sincere, ongoing change for the better
- Have excited interest in self-enhancing hobbies and projects
- Have a personal standard, albeit flexible, that applies to everyone and asks for accountability
- Appreciate feedback and can distinguish it from attempts to manipulate
- Relate only to partners with whom mutual love is possible
- Are strongly affected by your partner's behavior and take it as information
- See your partner as stimulating your excitement
- Let yourself feel anger, say "ouch" and embark upon a program of change
- Act out of agreement and negotiation

- Only do favors you choose to do (you can say no)
- Don't say yes to anything when you want to say no
- Honor intuitions and distinguish them from wishes
- Insist others' boundaries be as safe as your own
- Mostly feel secure and clear
- Are living a life that mostly approximates what you always wanted for yourself
- Decide how, to what extent, and how long you will be committed

2. Communicating through Conflict:

Four steps to handling a difficult conversation without confrontation

Loud voices, accusing words, cold shoulders, heated discussions. These are just a few signs of relationships and conversations that are on the verge of explosion. How we deal with these tough moments, in our actions and our language, is important—not only to our ability to maintain healthy relationships with others, but also to preserve our own peace of mind and self-esteem. Rose had a number of missed opportunities to have a difficult but necessary chat with her new so-called "family". If Rose had the strength to stand up for herself with healthy boundaries sooner, the outcome may not have changed, but her dignity would have been intact.

Here are four crucial communication skills and steps on how to manage a difficult conversation without detrimental confrontation.

Afterword

1. Speak directly (with the person)

Let's say you have had a disagreement, a misunderstanding, or even a fight with someone and you want to resolve it. It is best to speak directly with the other person involved. Ask for a time that is convenient for them, and agree to talk in person. It may take some courage to speak up and have a difficult conversation with someone, so practicing with a supportive friend may be helpful. Be convincing with your body language and your words. Remember that eighty percent of your communication will be non-verbal.

Practice being calm, as your tone of voice is also crucial in keeping a difficult conversation from heading toward a heated confrontation. This classic technique is extremely effective in expressing your feelings to another person. Speak your need this way: "I feel _____, when you _____could you please _____ (request)."

2. Soften the conversation

When discussions lead off in a negative and accusatory way, it has begun with a harsh start up. Psychologist, John Gottman, Ph.D., suggests using a "soft start up" to prevent major arguments when differences are present, by bringing up problems gently and without blame. His research reveals that 96% of the time you can predict the outcome of a fifteen-minute conversation based on the first three minutes of the interaction. Making a critical remark off-the- bat will only cause the other person to be defensive. Also, when sharing your opinion or request, use

"I" statements, as opposed to "You" statements, which only point out the problems and bad behavior you feel the other person has. For example, instead of saying, "You never listen to me" or "You always do (this or that)," say something like, "I feel frustrated/confused/not appreciated when (this) happens." Being sarcastic and using the terms "always" or "never" are likely to cause immediate defensiveness. Soften your next oppositional conversation, and if possible, begin it on a positive note. Discussions invariably end on the same note they begin.

3. Be a good listener

Perhaps one of the most precious and powerful gifts we can give another person is to really listen to them, to listen with quiet, fascinated attention, with our whole being, fully present. Try to withhold any judgment and do not interrupt when listening to another other person, while you are hearing all the facts and understanding his (or her) perspective. Ask questions to clarify his position or opinion. Don't get caught up in the trap of his games, by going around and around trying to prove who is right. Sometimes agreeing to disagree is the only option. Working toward mutual understanding and respect is the goal, in the midst of differing opinions. Being listened to and more importantly, being heard, is a fundamental need we all have.

4. Be solution-focused

In resolving conflicts, focus on one issue, one complaint, at a time. Try to agree on what the specific problem is, and then explore options to meet both people's needs. Avoiding conversations that may be difficult—because of hurt feelings or angry words spoken, may cause more problems. Each day that passes causes detachment for those involved and is a breeding ground for further misunderstandings. Also, remember the value of the relationship. Whether it is with a friend, a co-worker, a neighbor or a family member, focusing on the benefits of reconciliation may give you the boost you need to work through the problems. Calm communication during chaos, conflict, or crisis is a skill everyone needs. Communication is what connects all relationships. The words and actions we use can reveal a variety of thoughts and emotions, from love or excitement to anger and resentfulness.

3. Love is Caring *Not* Controlling

Signs & Solutions in Domestic Violence

What is Domestic Violence?

Domestic violence can be defined as a pattern of behavior in any relationship that is used to gain or maintain power and control over an intimate partner. The abuse may be emotional, physical, sexual, or include threats of actions that influence another person. This includes any behaviors that frighten, intimidate, terrorize, manipulate, hurt, humiliate, blame, injure or wound someone.

Rose's story is not about punches, but about put downs. Abuse doesn't have to be physical, although when people consider abuse they think of the bruises and the injuries. Mental and emotional abuse can be far crueler, leaving deeper wounds that are not always visible. Whether it was the father-in-law or Clay's brother, Rose was not emotionally safe around this family. Check out the signs below that evidenced Rose's abusive environment and make sure you are not allowing these toxic behaviors either.

Domestic violence can happen to anyone of any race, age, sexual orientation, religion or gender. It can happen to couples that are married, living together or who are dating. Domestic violence affects people of all socioeconomic backgrounds and education levels. While domestic violence can affect men, the large majority (85%) of its victims are women. Therefore, we're focusing on the most common type, where the male is the abuser in an intimate relationship.

You may be in an emotionally abusive relationship if your partner:

- Calls you names, insults you or continually criticizes you.
- Controls what you do, whom you see or talk to or where you go.
- Does not trust you and acts jealous or possessive.
- Tries to isolate you from family or friends.
- Monitors where you go, who you call and who you spend time with.
- Does not want you to work.
- Controls finances or refuses to share money.
- Punishes you by withholding affection.

Afterword

- Expects you to ask permission.
- Threatens to hurt you, the children, your family or your pets.
- Humiliates you in any way.

If you answered, "yes" to any one of these questions, you may be in an abusive relationship.

A Note about Older Battered Women

Older battered women are a nearly invisible, yet tragically sizable population and uniquely vulnerable to domestic violence. Older women are more likely to be bound by traditional and cultural ideology that prevents them from leaving an abusive spouse or from seeing themselves as a victim.

Older women are very often financially dependent on their abusive spouse and do not have access to the financial resources they need to leave an abusive relationship. Many older women find themselves isolated from their family, friends and community, due to their spouses' neglect and abuse. This is especially true because older women suffer greater rates of chronic illness, which makes them dependent upon their spouses or caregivers and thus, reluctant or unable to report abuse.

Getting Help

Here are some suggestions if you think you may be in a domestic violence situation:

S—Safe Places: think of safe places you can go, and safe people whom you trust.
A—Ask: ask for help, do not go it alone, a number of resources are available for support (crisis, emotional, legal).
F—Family: think of your family you are also protecting. Children are affected also.
E—Escape through planning: professionals will help you develop a detailed safety plan for leaving the relationship.
T—There is no excuse: remember there is no excuse for intimidation, control, and violence; do not be fooled by the cycle—the honeymoon phase of the apologies.
Y –You are valuable! Domestic violence is more than a relationship problem—it is a crime. Only you can take care of yourself and your children. Take the control back and seek help today.

Why Do Victims Stay?

Outsiders find it difficult to understand why anyone would stay in any type of abusive relationship. Victims are often blamed and labeled as weak and needy. Some people believe that if a woman stays in an abusive relationship she must somehow like it or need to be beaten to feel worthy. But the issue is more complex than simply leaving or staying. A woman may fear that the abuser will hurt her and her children or take her children away. She may have limited financial options.

She may blame herself. She may stay because she does not want to break up the family or she may stay for religious

Afterword

reasons. Also, she may still love her abuser and hope that things will get better. If you know someone who is being abused, be a good listener and supportive friend. Remind her that she and her children are worth better treatment. You may be able to help a victim understand her options. In turn, understand if she is reluctant to leave. She knows her abuser best and what options are safest.

How can I help a friend or family member who is being abused?

First, don't be afraid to let her know that you are concerned for her health and safety. Help your friend or family member recognize the abuse. Tell her you see what is going on and that you want to help.

Help them recognize that what is happening is not "normal" and that they deserve a healthy, non-violent relationship.

1. Acknowledge that she is in a very difficult and perhaps scary situation.

Let your friend or family member know that the abuse is not their fault. Reassure her that she is not alone and that there is help and support out there.

2. Be supportive.

Listen to your friend or family member. Remember that it may be difficult for her to talk about the abuse. Let her know that you are available to help whenever she may need it. What she needs most is someone who will believe and listen to her.

3. Be non-judgmental.

Respect your friend or family member's decisions. There are many reasons why victims stay in abusive relationships. She may leave and return to the relationship many times.

Do not criticize his or her decisions or try to guilt her. She will need your support even more during those times. Especially now, encourage her to participate in activities outside of the relationship with friends and family.

4. If she ends the relationship, continue to be supportive of her.

Even though the relationship was abusive, your friend or family member may still feel sad and lonely once it is over. She will need time to mourn the loss of the relationship and will especially need your support at that time. Help him or her to develop a safety plan—this is very important at this stage.

5. Encourage her to talk to people who can provide help and guidance.

Find a local domestic violence agency that provides counseling or support groups. Offer to go her to talk to family and friends. If she has to go to the police, court or a lawyer, offer to go along for moral support.

Afterword

6. Remember that you cannot "rescue" her.

Although it is difficult to see someone you care about get hurt, physically or emotionally, ultimately the person getting hurt has to be the one to decide that they want to do something about it. It's important for you to support her and help her find a way to safety and peace.

4. Six Simple Secrets of Great Relationships

What are the essential qualities of a great relationship? Communication and conflict resolution skills are certainly at the top of the list. But there are other skills and simple secrets to keep your relationship healthy and thriving. Below are six to consider. I bet you can see which were missing for Rose and Clay.

1. Share secrets

The best relationships involve friends who are open and honest with each other. They are not afraid to share parts of themselves with their partner. A strong sense of safety and trust is necessary in sharing secrets with each other—secrets that reveal your greatest interests, desires, dreams and disappointments. Being vulnerable increases intimacy and strengthens the relationship bond. Honor each other by being a safe place for your partner to share their secrets.

2. Cultivate common interests

Spending quality time together is crucial. This time can be with friends, dining out, attending a sporting event or cuddling together while watching a favorite movie. The event is not what is important. Just being together and doing something that you both enjoy will build a stronger relationship. Be creative in cultivating common interests. Inquire about your mate's hobbies and interests. Be open to learning something new, and share ideas with each other about common activities and interests. This will keep the fun in the friendship!

3. Pursue personal passions

As important as it is to spend quality time together, it is equally important to give your mate time to do something they enjoy independently. You must maintain a healthy sense of "self" in any relationship. Reflect on your own forgotten hobbies, and dive into personal pursuits that unleash your passions and unique gifts. Whether it's playing a musical instrument, baking or bowling, allow yourself some time to enjoy life apart from your partner. You will then feel renewing and refreshed as a couple!

4. Show support

Actions and words that show support of each other are keys to a great relationship. Find ways to validate your respect for each other. Remind him (or her) that he is a wonderful mate, husband and father (whichever applies). Lavish him with compliments, kind words that are often assumed and not spoken. When the other person fails or simply feels down or insecure, your encouragement is an opportunity to build them up by showing your sincere support. This is a blessing

Afterword

of a partnership—having your mate remind you of your greatness, in good times and in bad.

5. Forego the fairytale

When couples first get together, everything is new and exciting. They overlook the little annoying things the other person does and perhaps maintain a fairytale that all imperfections will disappear. Having unrealistic expectation about who the other person "will become" or how ideal the relationship will always be, destines it for disaster. Great relationships require ongoing effort based upon the love and values shared. Allow for shortcomings, and be flexible as you work to create and maintain a great—but real—relationship.

6. Release resentments

When you cannot let go of your guilt, regrets and resentments, there might as well be a chain connecting you to the past. Be willing to forgive and learn from relationship mistakes that will certainly occur. Living in a pain-filled past and harboring (what may be justified) resentments breeds a bacteria that stifles the growth of any relationship.

What resentments should you release?

5. Six Self Care Strategies for Women

Rose was the ultimate giver, from being a responsible and productive employee, to being a good friend, and eventually a loving wife. Self-care is the process of nurturing yourself. But in a fast-paced and often chaotic society, many women tend to put their own needs on the back burner. So many women constantly put everyone else first, allowing their own needs to suffer. Some women may even become resentful because their personal needs have been neglected.

Self-care for women is imperative. Follow these self-care strategies to help you take care of yourself and achieve balance your life

1. Recognize that self-care is not selfish

This concept of self-care refers to taking personal responsibility for one's physical, emotional, intellectual and spiritual health. Practicing self-care is preventative, not selfish. Yet the concept of making self-care a priority remains controversial. For most of us, if we do not take care of ourselves, no one else will. So, self-care is anything but selfish. When women don't make self-care a priority, they often feel like victims of something outside of themselves, in a position of restrictions and limitations. This prevents women from having rich and fulfilling lives.

2. Be your own best friend

What would happen if you treated yourself the same way you treat your best friend? You would likely be more attuned to your needs, your problems and your goals. You would be generous to yourself, as you are to others. You would love and honor your health and well-being. You would put aside all else to be your own best friend. One of the most important things you can do for your family and friends is to care for your own health. You can start by being a great friend to yourself today! And remember—the way you treat yourself sets the standard for others.

3. Spend time alone

Spending quality time alone is anything but lonely. Spending time alone allows the rest of the world to continue spinning while you rest, refuel and regroup. Time alone can be as simple as sitting quietly outdoors, reading a book at the park or sitting in your favorite comfortable chair with a cup of tea (having a favorite comfortable chair is essential!). And remember, being single does not mean you're weak. It means you are strong enough to wait for what you deserve. And you can choose for that to be a life partner or not.

4. Create supportive surroundings

Look around. Do you feel inspired by your surroundings, or do you feel tension and chaos? Create supportive surroundings by clearing the clutter of the stuff that drains you. Clear the clutter in your home, car or office. Clear clutter in relationships too, like one-sided relationships. Find a partner who also wants to redesign their life for the better. The support will be empowering for both of you, and a model for others around you. It will also help you balance the multiple roles you play as a woman.

5. Believe that saying "No" is OK

How many times have you said "yes," "sure" or "no problem" to a request, only to immediately regret your response? Have you ever committed your energy, time or money to a project, even though you have little or no desire to participate? Learning to say no is a skill, and it is a key self-care habit that can ignite your confidence and free your inner strength.

6. Rewrite your routine

If you can relate to the previous five suggestions, and you acknowledge the need to make changes in your life, then you may need to radically alter your daily or weekly routine. Begin by scheduling your own priorities into your routine first. When your own priorities are fulfilled, allow others' priorities on your schedule. Other people in your life may notice these changes. Share your plan with them, and explain your need for self-care. They will see the benefits of self-care reflected in your attitude and approach to life as well as the direct benefit they will receive from being in relationship with a more balanced you!

6. Time For Counseling?

Signs for Seeking Help

Have you ever felt like life is just too hard? Worried that you can't take the pressure, stress and anxiety anymore? I think

Afterword

Rose could have sought some counseling or other forms of support during those times when Clay just wasn't "getting" it. The problem was, she had too much trust in Clay, and maintained her faith that things would just get better.

Sometimes the stressors of life—whether situational or ongoing and dire—can be significant prompters to seek professional counseling. Everyone needs guidance, support and tools to navigate through taxing phases of life. If you or someone you know recognizes any of the following signs, it may be an indication to ask for help and seek professional counseling.

1. When you feel like you should

If it has already occurred to you that you need help and you would benefit from talking with someone to help tow you out of the ditch, then you should seek help. The greatest warning that we need additional assistance comes from our own sense of need. Even if you cannot identify the cause of your distress, you may feel an overwhelming need to remove it. A supportive counselor or therapist can help pinpoint the issues that keep you stuck and facilitate a plan for renewal. Asking for help is a significant step in the right direction.

2. When family friction is high

Elevated stress from family friction is an invitation to seek outside help. In today's culture of divorce, single-parenting and blended families, the challenge of maintaining harmony in our homes has become difficult and complex.

Today's families also have temptations brought on by the internet, such as gambling, pornography or any number of other luring enticements that cater to our vulnerabilities. If you want better conflict resolution skills, parenting skills or tips to manage your own stress, remember, you do not have to solve your dilemmas by yourself. Caring professionals with experience in problematical family issues can help.

3. When grief lingers

Grief is painful. When grief is complicated or suppressed it can linger and cause unbearable effects on our lives. People commonly experience painful grief over losing a loved one, but grief can result from events as well. Disenfranchised grief reflects a loss that cannot be openly acknowledged, publicly mourned or socially supported. Examples of this can be failed dreams, failed relationships or even failed expectations. It is healthy to grieve losses in your life but if grief overtakes you and you cannot move on after a period of time, find support through individual counseling, support groups or both.

4. When denial has failed

When attempts at escaping your problems have failed, and when you have become tired of being sick and tired, you can make a new decision and take a new direction. There comes a time to accept the realities of your sorrow and uncover the make-believe shelter your denial provides. Maybe you're trading one painful way of life for another.

Afterword

It's common for people in denial. Many mask their problems by feeding their addictions to alcohol, drugs, sex or even shopping. When denial has had its last day as the epicenter of your life, your healing can begin.

5. When being controlled

If you are in any type of relationship where you are manipulated, dominated or controlled, then you need help. If you believe your actions, your involvements, your finances or any part of your lifestyle has limited freedom due to someone placing restrictions on you, you should seek help. You can discover healthier ways of coping and for thriving. Do not let your valuable life slip into seclusion and submission. Rage and resentment can build up, and you can find yourself in what seems like a trapped position. Professional help is available, ready to offer you avenues of strength, safety and of success.

6. When confronted with crisis

Survivors of traumatic events are frequently in such a state of shock that simply enduring each day becomes the primary task. Examples of traumatic events could include a sudden family death, a spouse announcing an affair or learning that a child that has been arrested. A crisis or critical incident is any incident that challenges your normal coping skills. If you don't have support systems, or don't know of resources for recovery, the crisis can be alarming and intense. Skilled professionals can guide you through the journey of recovery.

7. When surrounded in sadness

If your life feels dark and lonely and you feel like you are surrounded by sadness, then there is a great indication that you could benefit from counseling. Depression is more than feeling "blue" or having a bad day. Being depressed is like having the sun no longer shine on your soul. Your life may feel hollow. You may feel invisible. You may feel hope and joy are out of reach. If you have no interest in normal or fun activities or are very tired but sleep does not make the emotional or physical pain go away, don't wait another day before asking for help.

7. The Good News About Stress

Five facts of the benefits of stress:

Have you ever felt overwhelmed, tired, anxious or frustrated like Rose? Everyone encounters stressful circumstances most every day. Stress is a natural reaction of your mind and body to external demands. The good news is that stress can also provide an invitation to improve your life and recognizing stress is an opportunity for individual growth and positive change. Stress is actually essential to life. It is the excessive or unresolved stress that results in negative consequences. Rose has indeed chosen to live the lessons and she keeps growing from her tragic marriage. It may be time to move forward for you—no matter what stress you have survived. The key is how you believe, perceive and react to the various less-than-desirable circumstances of everyday life.

Afterword

Below are five, perhaps surprising, ways that stress can actually help you and increase the satisfaction of your life:

1. It Gets your attention

Noticing stress in your life serves as a warning sign—a waving, glowing red flag that something in your life may not be working its best. How do you first recognize stress in your life? You may experience symptoms of stress either physically, emotionally or behaviorally. Some people first recognize stress when they detect a headache or backache. For others, they may easily become impatient, snappy, and snippy.

Others may notice the stress in one area of their lives only when it has leaked into or even barraged other areas, much like dangerous and scattering cancer cells. Experiencing excessive stress can get your attention by unveiling a number of issues; including lack of life balance, unhealthy relationships, or deteriorating health problems, to name a few. Pay attention to these. Take note of the warning signs that your stress level may be climbing, and do something about it today.

2. It reveals core needs

Think of the last time you had a stressful day. One person's experience of stress may be very different than another person's. This is because as individuals we have different core needs. When these needs are not being met, stress soon follows. If one spouse, for example, has a core need of order, and the other does not share in this need or try to meet that need, anxiety and stress can be a daily irritation. Or, if one person in a group has a core need for planning and scheduling and the rest of the group prefers to "wing it," the person who needs certainty will definitely feel stress. It is important to identify your core needs and acknowledge the link between unmet needs and stress. Therefore, when you recognize your core needs are not being met in one way, you can choose a different way to get them met.

3. It readjusts your expectations

We are full of expectations—lots of expectations. Some we are consciously aware of and many others, we are not. Expectations are always there in the background of our daily experiences however. They are a common source of stress in our lives, creating emotional distress, relationship conflicts, misunderstandings, and many other repeated problems. Expectations produce stress in two main ways. Some are unrealistic or untrue, like the blissful and problem free expectations that newlyweds encounter. Others expectations are those of which we are completely unaware, like the belief that life or people will be fair. This blindness will surely lead to stress and strain. When we harbor expectations that are too high, we set ourselves up for failure. The stress resulting from this disappointment serves as an opportunity to readjust our expectations—of ourselves, and of others.

4. It reminds us of personal responsibility

Stressful experiences serve as reminders of what you can control and what you cannot control. You are probably

Afterword

keenly aware you cannot control other people—whether family, friends or coworkers. Their actions can disappoint us, betray us or discourage us on a regular basis if we allow them to. We have no control over what another person ultimately does. We can only control our response to them. This kind of stress serves as a distinctive reminder to take personal responsibility for our choices. The stress encountered from other people's actions, or inactions, can sometimes feel like it is eating us alive. It is unfortunate when we fail to see our reaction choices as options for immediate stress management. Circumstances may be beyond our control, but there are many options for how to deal with, or adjust to them, that can cause less stress. Begin taking responsibility for your choices that contribute to, or minimize, your stress today!

5. It leads to growth!

Life is never stagnating, and this is a good thing. Change is constant. It is constant in relationships, in the environment, and in the work force. The burden of stress resulting from change is common in our culture today. As leadership expert and motivational speaker John Maxwell puts it, "Change always involves growth." Through the growing pains of adjusting to aging and to navigating through other life transitions, experiencing some degree of stress is normal.

Through disappointments, loss, and the fact that we live in an uncertain world, stress is normal as well. Through this stress and change, we grow and persevere by learning new ways to accommodate, to develop patience, to mature, and to practice lessons learned. Any given circumstance of stress will change with time—or we can choose to change ourselves.

The good news about stress here is…it always leads to growth. Capture your opportunities for growth for whatever current stressors it seems are managing you.

Most importantly, look back to the growth that has made you who you are today—a beautiful, fragrant rose, reaching for the sky; rising above the tiny, insignificant thorns below.

Susan Gillpatrick, M.Ed., LPC, CTS, CATSM, CEAP

As Crisis Management Specialist with Centerstone, www.Centerstone.org, the nation's largest behavioral health organization, Susan Gillpatrick leads a variety of comprehensive crisis prevention and response programs, personal and professional growth trainings, as well as provides immediate on-site post-incident behavioral health care (CISM) after any traumatic event in the workplace. Susan is a licensed professional counselor and mental health service provider, a Workplace Conflict Mediator, Certified Trauma Specialist and a board certified expert in traumatic stress. A wellness expert, speaker and published author, Susan has a Master of Education in Human Development Counseling from Vanderbilt University and has worked in the field of Behavioral Health for more than twenty years. Susan can be reached at susan.gillpatrick@centerstone.org

Terri Merryman Writer, Publicist

Award-winning writer Terri Merryman has ducked rifle fire, lived in an Israeli colony, and moved into a Russian village to anchor and report on important news stories. She's interviewed subjects as volatile as Shimon Peres and Newt Gingrich and as genteel as Lena Horne and Nancy Reagan, but her belief that everyone has at least one unique and interesting story to share, has never waned.

Her career has put her in the roles of news anchor, reporter, talk show host, and even associate producer for the top-rated *Survivor Reunion* reality show. Terri has anchored in Nashville, Los Angeles, Philadelphia, Miami and Atlanta and has reported for NBC's morning syndicated show *Real Life*.

Working in Los Angeles placed Terri in the middle of the Hollywood action at Paramount and at the famed CBS Television City Studios. It was the best of all worlds for this movie and entertainment buff who coached young Reese Witherspoon when she began her Oscar-winning acting career. Terri is currently ghostwriting several books and serves as a coach, publicist and consultant to aspiring actors, authors, entertainers, and reporters. She writes from the peace and tranquility of her horse farm overlooking the Cumberland River near Lebanon, Tennessee.

www.ingramcontent.com/pod-product-compliance
Lightning Source LLC
Chambersburg PA
CBHW031143160426
43193CB00008B/239